P9-BZK-090

INVERTED FLIGHT

INVERTED FLIGHT

A Collection of Verse

Don Mercer
Rustic 41

Copyright © 2004 by H. G. "Don" Mercer, Rustic 41.

ISBN :   Hardcover   1-4134-4897-6
           Softcover   1-4134-4896-8

All rights reserved. No part of this book may be reproduced or transmitted in
any form or by any means, electronic or mechanical, including photocopying,
recording, or by any information storage and retrieval system, without permission
in writing from the copyright owner.

This book was printed in the United States of America.

To order additional copies of this book, contact:
Xlibris Corporation
1-888-795-4274
www.Xlibris.com
Orders@Xlibris.com
20009

CONTENTS

EULOGY TO LIEUTENANT COLONEL DONALD H. HAGLE, USAF (RETIRED) "BEAGLE"—RUSTIC 40

THOUGHTS ON LIFE

THE WAR IN SOUTHEAST ASIA

ON SEPTEMBER 11TH

ALASKA

MORE ON LIFE

In Memory

of

Lt. Col. Donald H. Hagle, United States Air Force

Call Sign over Cambodia 1970-71: Rustic 40

Captain John William "Jack" Kennedy, Brother Rat,
Virginia Military Institute

Call Sign: Jake 23

Missing In Action on August 16, 1971,
in the Republic of Vietnam
Subsequently Confirmed as Killed in Action
The Wall: Panel 03W—Line 132

and

In Honor

of

Captain Jean C. Roth, United States Army Nurse Corps
Service at Chu Lai, RVN, 1967-68

_____

First Lieutenant Robert C. Leibecke, Jr., United States Army,
101st Airborne Division
Brother Rat, VMI
Service in I Corps, RVN, 1970-71

_____

The Rustics

Foreword

On April 30, 1970 a new phase in the Vietnam War began. The incursion of U.S. forces into Cambodia was ordered by President Nixon to destroy large areas of supplies, hidden in the jungles that had been assembled by North Vietnam over the years to support its war against the south. This incursion was the precursor of the formation of a special top-secret U.S. task force— a group of Air Force pilots called "forward air controllers", flying out of Vietnam and over Cambodia. The U.S. ground forces withdrew after only 60 days. But this left the Cambodian government, which had given the U.S. permission to come into their country, vulnerable to the wrath of the North Vietnamese Army. The task force was specifically created to help Cambodia in its struggle against the communist forces—to provide U.S. air support for the Cambodian Army units.

This task force was known as the "Rustics". Their mission was to provide continuous air coverage of Cambodia, 24 hours a day and seven days a week, ready to call for and direct U.S. fighter bombers stationed in Vietnam to support the Cambodian army. The contingent of the Rustic task force that provided this support during the nighttime hours became known as the Night Rustics. I had the honor of commanding this group of young pilots from December 1970 until we were disbanded in September 1971. It also brought to me the privilege of flying and fighting with, and knowing, Don Mercer.

Don Mercer was a Night Rustic. A large part of the poetry he offers here has been inspired by the events and emotions of the year Don spent in Vietnam serving both his own country as well as the Cambodian nation. Many of the poems he has herein provided us include a prominent appreciation for his love of flying, for his comrades in arms, the honor of serving, and for beloved comrades who were lost.

But Don's poetry is not only about flying and war. He has included many delightful poems of life, family, patriotism, and Alaska—a state I have visited as well, and a state you cannot visit without being totally captured by its beauty. Knowing Don as I do, I recognize the repertoire presented here is an honest reflection of himself, his own life experiences, thoughts, and his broad interests. Imbedded in Don's spirit is a deep love for life, his country, his friends, and his marvelous family.

Don has had a full life and many varied and unique experiences, well beyond that of the common person. He has captured a number of these experiences in this book, hoping that someway he might be able to share just a bit of his exhilaration with the reader.

As you read these works, carry closely with you the thought that the poetry is a true reflection of Don's soul. It will enrich your reading experience.

Richard (Dick) Roberds
Colonel, USAF (Retired)
Harrisonburg, Virginia
May 2003

Preface

As it happened, Don Hagle, a fellow pilot in Southeast Asia, died as I was about to board the first of several planes en route to Alaska in July, 2001. I was to join there with three other men whom I'd come to know from my having flown F-105's, years ago, with the 149th Tactical Fighter Squadron.

Don Hagle, "Beagle," was a great friend with whom I'd flown in the skies over Cambodia in 1970-71 during the war. So I put the time when traveling to Alaska to good use and, with much reflection, penned "Passing the Test—The Best of the Best," a eulogy that was read by his sister at his funeral. If that is the best poem that I ever write, I accept it readily as Don deserved only the best. He, like many Americans whom I have had the good fortune to know, served our country with distinction.

With my left arm in a cast, for a change riding in the back seat of a general aviation plane, I flew for most of the next two weeks over the grandness that is Alaska. I found myself devoting a great deal of thought to a variety of issues—family, friends, country and religion, to name but a few. That time, as with my return to Southeast Asia—Cambodia, Vietnam and Thailand—in 1999, proved to be trips of a lifetime.

Thus, began my efforts at verse as I have always enjoyed writing. The attacks on September 11th awakened painful feelings and served as the impetus for a few of my poems. The poems devoted to the time spent in Vietnam and missions flown over Cambodia address, in many cases, little known battles and aspects of that war.

While I kept a journal of much that took place during my 12 month tour based at Bien Hoa, Republic of Vietnam, and of our unit's flying in Cambodia, I hope that my verse can far better express some of the range of emotions that prevailed throughout that period of my life. As I am confident is the case with all who have served in combat, many of the emotions from that period will last my lifetime.

As with most military, government and aviation topics, there is a language unto itself. Suffice it to say, the experience in Southeast Asia and with flying came with an abundance of distinct nomenclature for everything from ordnance to organizations. In any event, I have provided some limited comments and footnotes that may hopefully be of assistance.

I have always enjoyed on occasion flying upside down and looking at the world beneath as the cover reflects. Webster's Dictionary also defines "inverted" as "to turn inward." Thus, the title: *Inverted Flight.*

My verse, therefore, covers a wide swath of life as I have known it. It represents who I am now and have been, speaks to God's greatness as I believe it to be, and seeks to honor a number of people.

Virginia Beach, VA
February 1, 2004

EULOGY TO LIEUTENANT COLONEL DONALD H. HAGLE, USAF (RETIRED) "BEAGLE"—RUSTIC 40

Passing the Test—
The Best of the Best

Many years ago in a far away land
    The challenge was that of becoming a man.
We were young and invincible, true to a soul,
    As pilots and FACs we suffered no fools.

Among us were those who were young and brave,
    Daring and cunning with lives to be saved.
We flew at night and enjoyed new found rigors;
    All meeting the challenge with great vim and vigor.

Through darkness, weather, dimmed lights, bright gunfire;
    All met the schedule, though however sometimes dire.
No one shirked their duty for missions of ease,
    As we loved life to the limit and fought for allies to be free.

New found friends in Cambodia and Vietnam,
    That were sure to remain with us for a lifetime.
There were among us young men who were best;
    Harris, Sovich, Baker, Jones and all of the rest.

Perry and Greene, "Casper" and "Goose;"
    Men who fought valiantly not wanting to lose.
There were Lemke, Gibbar, Thrower, Lancaster and Litton,
    Dekoker, Bell, Case, Hopkins and Boston,

Gonzalez, Casey, Driskill—None are forgotten;
    America's sons—What they call a cross section;
Messer, Hull and Virtue—Along with a few;
    All led by Roberds, young also but true.

Known by monikers most came to be called:
    "Slapper", "Redeye", "Stump", "Over", "Zeke" and "Doc" Pells;
But the best of the best was a lieutenant called "Beagle;"
    To some known as Don and others as Dee.
He loved more than most to fly like an eagle.

As a young man he yearned to join with the sky;
    To be free, to be bold, to learn how to fly.
To remain on the ground would be but a drag;
    So he worked with the crop dusters, holding the flag.

And he flew in the hopper when day's work was done,
    So as a young man he could have the most fun.
He joined the U. S. Air Force, following his father;
    To serve God and country, family and all others.

As I sit here today with the clouds passing by,
    I know "Beagle" is watching us now from on high.
Not a day will go by that we won't say hi,
    To our departed brother, among the first to go by.

But today our need is for respect and goodby,
    To recall all the fun we had long ago,
To help us arise from a day that is low.
    And for others most fortunate spending more time with him,
His family and Lynette, I'd rather be them.

Our time together was all too short,
    But far better than most when away from port.
Don had a career in the Air Force, 'tis true,
    He wore the uniform—True to the Blue.

But for us here today we should only recall why
    Don's purpose in life was to love and to fly.
The missions he flew in that far away land,
    Are forgotten by some, only known to few hands.

He flew cover and fought battles, more than a few;
    Throwing care to the wind, for among us he knew
That our mission was best among those who were there,
    While to most unknown, we all came to dare
For the weary Cambodians who needed our care.

Many others died there as surely we could;
    But God has a plan if only we would
Come to understand why we're here today
    When good men like Don are taken away.

Don saved many lives while taking the test,
    He, with us all, tried to save all the rest.
While that war has been muddled, it was clear to us all;
    While others stood short—To a man we stand tall.

A confusing war to most in our land,
    Our job was simple—To give but a hand.
Don flew many missions across the fence;
    'Cross miles of jungle, green and so dense,

To provide the hand that held the bright light;
    He braved darkness and weather, carrying the fight into night;
To those that would torture and come to oppress;
    For that long year together, he knew little rest;

To hit the Khmer Rouge again and again
    He returned for more missions, to fly and to win.

I had the great honor of sitting beside
   Rustic Four Zero as we went on those rides.
Both in left seat and right seat on those long ago missions,
   We not only believed, but had then a vision:

Hoping men would be free and life would be fair;
   Taking risks as young men do, as if on a dare.
The adrenalin rushed when our friends called in trouble;
   Don would fly to the scene, his efforts yet doubled.

That in the blink of an eye, it seems now but yesterday
   When Don rode into battle, leading the way.
To have known Don the longest must surely be best;
   But we got back together, long after the test.

Of young men who flew as brother with brother,
   We all but too late found one another.
Only a few years ago we got back together
   To reminisce and to hope that it all had been better.

For that far away land we still call our home;
   Not ground now, but a unit of men—none alone.
We were Rustics so many nights long ago,
   Many yesterdays past when we flew—Oh! So low.

Warriors all, but true lovers of peace;
   We wanted to win, but some settled for least.
Don was then with us, a leader of men—
   A long time ago—Away back then.

Young and heroic as were the rest,
>He led the way when we passed the test.
Our job today is no longer to fight,
>But to recall again those long ago nights

When young men like Don were wont to be bold,
>So that others like us may now live to be old.
But perhaps the best lesson to be learned from my brother:
>Is to help other people and love one another.

He returned to America and flew the F-4;
>To fly low, to fly fast and help many more.
As his log entries ended with T-43's,
>Helping train more men and women that others may be free.

A great pilot, honest and wonderful friend;
>Our loss is now reckoned with today in the end.
And among us Don's memory will always last,
>For indeed, for us, his life passed too fast.

For he was among the Best of the Best
>As he rapidly bounded past the test.
Those years now are fading into the past;
>Don's among those to go, but far from the last

Of pilots and others who desire to be free;
>Who believe in God and trust in Thee.
'Twas a twist of fate to have been me,
>'Twas only a fleeting moment in time,
The Reward—Don Hagle—a good friend of mine.

Memories to be treasured, thoughts to be saved—
    In the land of the free, our home of the brave.
The pictures we took then today have a blank,
    A brother is gone—But to Him we give thanks.

Of some things we are certain, no need to take pause;
    Don's life has great meaning, even in loss.
There was never a doubt of his passing the test;
    For Don Hagle was among the Best of the Best.

THOUGHTS ON LIFE

Up in the Sky

To soar and fly like birds on high;
To roll and turn and dive;

To float along as clouds go by;
Makes me feel so alive.

When I was but a boy so young;
To join the Air Force Blue

Was my desire that proved not wrong
Made lifelong friends, we flew

Many kinds of planes, 'twas grand;
Some fast and some so slow;

Was then I came to understand
Why God has let us go

In His backyard up in the sky
Where only birds had flown;

A sense of peace as we flew high;
Where quietude is sown;

'Tis there I find the beauty all
Of life and serenity dear;

As I grow older near the call
Hope that heaven is here.

Neighbors

Of all the great neighbors we've enjoyed over the years, Colonel
Dick Haislip, USMC (Retired), and his lovely wife, Mary, set
the standard for those who are not only good but for those
singular neighbors who are truly outstanding. As a couple
Dick and Mary, while adoring each other, raise the bars
for the true meaning of marriage and what it is to
be gracious.

There are neighbors—gracious and fine;
And others not so nice;
Some who offer dinner and wine;
And those who are like ice.

Then you find a few special ones
Unlike some you avoid;
Secure as friends, while having fun;
Not dull or jokes devoid.

Those are the ones—become so dear;
Like family and so linked;
And on the block where they are near;
With them you are in sync.

You love to hear about their kids;
And best—the grandchildren;
Important things the young ones did;
The how, why, where and when.

Those neighbors are like specks of gold;
They're difficult to find;
So nice to bond as all grow old;
So rare—one's of a kind.

Time Flies By

Yesterday's gone, we can't get it back.
The future's ahead and for it we pack.

Best not to revel in yesterday's past;
But to live for today, for it won't last.

Time flies by as we grow and get older;
When younger was better to be all the bolder.

As we gain in years—get set in our ways;
The summer of life turns to autumn's days.

We lose a few friends along life's short way;
All the more reason to value today;

'Cause time passes by and waits for no man;
So seize life—and live it—best while you can.

'Tis said when you have health—you have it all.
While you savor the good life—have a ball!

Ride the waves of time as hours and days go by;
Live life to the fullest asking not why.

Time halts for no one—of that to be sure.
For days wasted and lost—absolutely no cure!

Gone over the dam like water gone past;
So use time wisely—while for you time, it lasts!

Beware of Sharks

Dedicated to my daughter, Cheerie, who, since shark attacks at
Sandbridge, VA, on September 1, 2001, and at Avon, NC, on
September 3, 2001, both of which were unfortunately fatal, has
a greatly diminished desire to play in the Atlantic Ocean.

Do you want a body part—a favorite perhaps to choose?
    Or rather let a hungry shark decide what you will lose?
Tiger, bull or hammerhead—it really makes no difference!
    They're just voracious critters from the deep—bites making
      little sense.

The randomness, with no warning, makes it all the more scary;
    For folks like you and me, when wading becomes quite leery.
I think I'll again go fly in the sky, or lay relaxing on the sand;
    'Cause those fins that skim just above the surface—may
      sacrifice a hand!

But in the sky as you float along, I never ever heard
    Of things like sharks, for, No indeed! There are no man-eating birds.
So I think I'll still go to the beach—to soak up all that sun;
    Build sand castles, play volleyball, and enjoy all that great fun.

But when it comes to getting wet—it's right back to the pool;
    'Cause I like my parts—Can't see those sharks—think I am not a fool!
There may really be little reason for these recent attacks by sharks;
    On the other hand wouldn't blame them much for leaving
      their grizzly marks.

For we've fouled the rivers and oceans for all too many years;
    And if sharks are of high intelligence—their message may be real clear:
Leave enough fish in the ocean deep for those sharks to seek and score;
    And if they have small fishes out there, they'll stay far away
        from our shores.

But if we continue to over fish, and on the oceans but place a strain;
    Then can't blame them—those sleek gray streaks—for adding
        us to their food chain.
Come to think of it—'tis not much fun to be considered just a course
    For those teethy beasts may now only see us as food—just
        another source.

And do not wear shiny objects—may to them look just like scales;
    And if you're in the water, try not to thrash and flail.
They're not the type you want to attract—so get out if you are bleeding;
    To elude them at all times, but most certainly when they are feeding.

So avoid the early morning and all evenings but for sure;
    'Cause those are just the times when my Dad said to cast my lure.
And here's another thought, makes plenty sense to me—
    Stay far from fishing piers, where parts of fish are freed.

So the moral of this story is like many things in life—
    Just assessing risk against reward to minimize the strife.
The ocean's been their playground for millions of years gone nigh
    So I think I'll just sit on the beach awhile, and wave as those
        sharks go by.

So use some care and common sense, and when in the water take pause;
    But there's certainly no need for us today to make killing
        sharks a cause.

Blue Ridge Morn

The Blue Ridge Mountains of Virginia;
So much beauty to behold.
Just like the Smokies in North Carolina;
God's mountains—Oh! So old.

As the mist surrounds the ridge lines;
You can see for miles and miles;
O'er evergreens and southern pines;
Sun rising in awhile.

As the rays from the east start shining;
Most animals starting to stir;
The mist begins evaporating;
Look closely for flashes of fur.

The sun ascends as the world turns;
Birds singing to beat the band;
Beads of moisture falling from the ferns;
'Tis God's country and His land.

Up Afton Mountain as you climb;
The shadows peel away;
Every morn, as if immortal time;
When skies are clear, bringing light of day.

Such wonders of His majesty;
Surround us one and all.
So take the time to view the beauty;
In God's magnificent halls.

Dogwoods, hickories, maples and oaks;
Resplendent in the Fall.
Autumn's foliage, brilliant when awoke;
Crossing hillsides as it crawls.

From glistening reds to yellows;
And orange before turns brown.
The colors of God's forest bellows;
'Fore taking winter's frown.

Fall is a marvelous season;
'Tis nice to get about.
And for us all, the more reason;
Seek to understand God's clout.

For Noelle on Your 21st Birthday

Congratulations, Happy Birthday, your Twenty First is here;
   A wonderful day, one when it's finally legal to drink beer.
We've seen you grow so wonderfully, over all the years gone by;
   While life has not been sometimes clear, you've faced it eye to eye.

Regardless of trials and tribulations, we've always held you dear;
   We love to see you travel, but 'tis always best when you're near.
We want to see you spread your wings and fly as it was meant;
   But always remember through your life, it's with our love you're sent.

We're sure that there'll be problems, for life's not always fair;
   But we'll always be here for you, as our love for you is rare.
So go now that you're twenty-one and enjoy life to the fullest;
   Having fun with new friends, traveling far, but we're still as if closest.

To you when you are away from home, we'll always share your joy;
   No matter how hard you try, it will be hard for you to annoy
Those of us who love you most, who want for you the best;
   So that you may enjoy throughout your life—certainly all the rest;

The wonders as you grow older, that only good things will come
   your way;
   That o'er the years ahead you'll have a great future, both at
   home and when away.
So for today with friends and family, here to celebrate;
   We wish you well, with all our love, twenty-one years since
   that grand date.

When you first joined with our lives, giving joy and so much fun;
    You, with your two younger sisters, are like to us the sun.
And when life's storms, on the horizon, or last awhile, for days;
    Remember those good experiences that will come 'round
    again to stay.

For life's a lot like the weather: storms, clouds, wind, rain and sleet;
    Just try to avoid the hurricanes and tornadoes—those you
    don't want to meet.
But surely as the bright day arrives, shortly after the dark night;
    Your skies in life will clear for sure, leaving only but delight.

For those that do not find this, in life to be just so;
    Are only those who are negative or choose only to look below.
As you've often heard the glass is half empty, or half full, as you so choose;
    But to those who see half empty, they are generally the first to lose.

Try always in life to see the glass, at worst, at least half full or more;
    And life will release its treasures to you, as from its bounteous store.
So keep your head raised high, and for those blue skies seek;
    And then just as when the day arrives, you'll need only 'round to peek

At all the wonderful joys life holds: family, friends and love;
    God's beauties in this world of ours as He looks down from above.
So put aside for those rainy days as, indeed, they will appear;
    So that when they are upon you, you'll only need but steer

Again to those bright days ahead, that will always reappear
    To those who work hard seeking them, to reach those days we
    hold so dear.
And as you go along in life, only try but to recall;
    Advice we've given, what's best for you, so that you may never fall.

But if you stumble, we'll be here, as parents doing our best;
    So from this point go forward, to enjoy your life—the rest.
And if you hold these tidbits, and follow your moral compass high;
    You'll face the wind, much stronger, perhaps with but a sigh;

You'll stand upright, shoulders back, head up, and take life as it comes;
    Whether far away in distant lands or with us here at home.
So go forth now and seek to moderate those joys and sorrows, too;
    Try to smooth out life's sharp edges, so you'll only see the blue

Of skies so bright and days so clear you'll do nothing but enjoy;
    If you work hard when you need to—life will be but a wonderful toy
That you can throw about, play at it and with others so behold;
    That when work is done, you can savor all good things as you grow old.

But you are young today, and we're here with you to enjoy, to celebrate;
    Your coming of age, enjoying life to the hilt, on this, a wonderful date.

Physical Therapy

After experiencing my distal biceps tendon in my left arm being severed in July, 2001, three months of physical therapy following surgery finally enabled me to swing a golf club again in November. Unfortunately, the surgery attaching the tendon did not slow my swing or improve my game.

As you get somewhat older and parts start to wear;
  Your body gets sorer and occasionally tears;
After seeing the doctor—perhaps surgery had;
  Next stop's physical therapy—it's not all that bad.

Start stretching and pulling—while avoiding the pain;
  Maybe rolling a sphere—seeing some with a cane;
Placing your arm or body in a whirlpool bath;
  With good physical therapy as the aftermath.

Using exercise machines and throwing a ball;
  Pushing a large round cylinder up and down walls;
Watching as others walk injured around the room;
  Seeing some improving helps minimize the gloom.

Using a timer, keep track of each exercise;
  First working range of motion—now strength on the rise;
Lifting weights, starting out with pastel ones so small;
  Then moving to ones heavier, isn't this a ball?

Having scar tissue pinched, more the better to heal;
  Physical therapy's an art—today quite the deal.
It's amazing to me: only months past the pain;
  Now that recovery's most complete—like new again!

Snowfall

For my daughter, Erin, whose love of winter skiing is unsurpassed.

First flakes of snow upon the ground
Announce that winter's here;

Warmth of summer no longer found;
Cold days of winter—clear.

To see the snow fall—crystals white:
A beauty to behold;

Ground covered fresh—wondrous delight;
And see your breath when cold.

The joy of seeing snowfall 'round
With children all in glee;

Blades of green grass no longer found;
Covered for none to see.

The snowflakes are like gold to kids
To frolic and play in.

It's time to get the skates and sleds;
See all those youths with grins.

So look to winter with a smile;
It's fun to laugh and ski.

With snow affording grand lifestyle
For folks like you and me.

THE WAR IN
SOUTHEAST ASIA

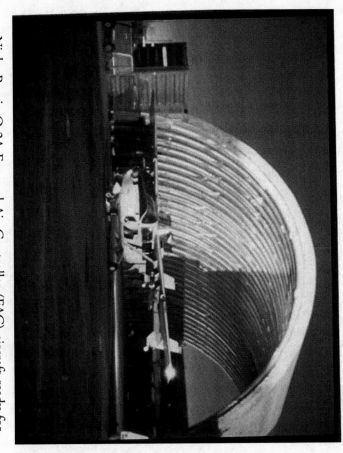

Night Rustic O-2A Forward Air Controller (FAC) aircraft ready for night launch from Bien Hoa Air Base, Republic of Vietnam (RVN), 1971

Destination: Cambodia

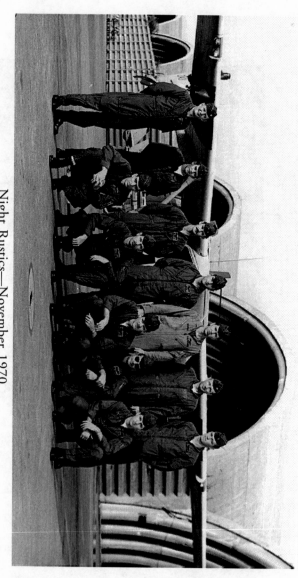

Night Rustics—November 1970

Standing, L-R: Jim Lester (III DASC Task Force Commander), Mick Gibbar, Don Hagle, Drake Greene, Don Mercer, Jim Hetherington (O-2 Night Rustic Commander), and Bob Messer. Front Row, L-R: John Litton, Dave Dekoker, Bill Lemke, Tom Canter, and Wayne Baker.

Night Rustics—June 1971

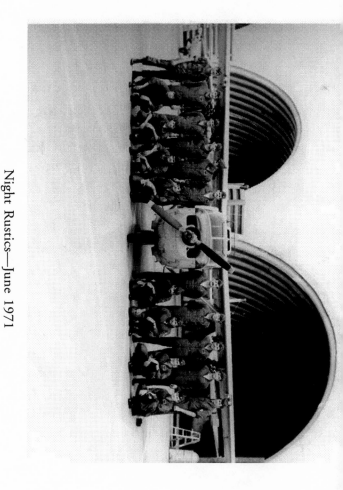

Standing, L-R: Jack Koppin (19th TASS Task Force Deputy Commander), Dick Roberds (O-2 Night Rustic Commander), Larry Knox, Bob Harris, Drake Greene, Tom Jones, Ron Grattopp, Blake Lancaster, Merle Shields, Wendell Pells, and Don Mercer. Front Row, L-R: Damon Gonzalez, Wayne Baker, Mick Gibbar, Steve Hopkins, Tom Canter, Jack Bowen, Chuck Casey, and Paul Dimmick.

Friends

Dedicated to Captain John William "Jack" Kennedy, my Brother Rat, Class of 1969, Virginia Military Institute, and fellow O-2A Forward Air Controller (FAC). Jack was listed as Missing In Action (MIA) on August 16, 1971, in the Republic of Vietnam. Thanks to efforts by the Joint Task Force and many others, the crash site of his aircraft was located over two decades later in Quang Tin, RVN. His remains were subsequently identified, with interment at Arlington National Cemetery on August 2, 1996. The Wall: Panel 03W—Line 132.

When I was young and played outdoors;
"Friends" was the word oft used.

But as I grew with years the more;
I found the term abused.

For when I flew in combat long
I learned the true intent

Of "friends," had been most times used wrong;
For then I had a glint:

For there my "friends"—willing to give;
Their lives for others then;

So other "friends" could then but live;
And since remember when;

Those who gave their lives for others;
　　Are true heroes for me;

And "friends" of all, thanks to mothers;
　　Who raised them but to see;

That "friends" are those who sacrifice;
　　Their all when called upon;

They're willing to give precious life;
　　Those "friends" were paragons.

For the Nurses

Dedicated to the nurses who served in Southeast Asia and especially to my sister-in-law, Jean C. Roth, who served in I Corps in 1967-68 as an Army operating room nurse with the Second Surgical Hospital at Chu Lai, Republic of Vietnam, and to her friend Pat Walsh, a State Department nurse who worked at Danang, RVN.

Not in thousands was their number;
Who served our country well.
But like many of the men there;
A few came to know death's knell.

In the thick of it were nurses;
Who tended to the pain;
Of broken bodies, full of holes;
So many with blood stains.

They tended o'er the abattoir;
As men from battle came;
Parting with pieces of their souls;
As angels, they became.

Saving lives and healing wounded;
While putting in long hours.
Through kindness, skill, and dedication;
They gave of their great power.

'Tis sad to note that from it all;
So many suffer now.
Like others in the aftermath;
Came to ponder, why and how.

Those nurses made such sacrifice;
So others would get well.
Now our country, only decades later;
Appreciates their suffering: 'tis parallel.

Departure

Dedicated to my Brother Rats who served in Southeast Asia and especially the four who did not live to return: Thomas G. Blair, Jr.; Arthur L. Galloway, Jr.; John W. Kennedy; and Franklin W. Webb

'Twas a story in itself, as we gathered there that day,
A four engine jet readying for boarding, near the long runway.
It was September, Nineteen Seventy, the 10th as I vividly recall;
For each of us who arrived there, to Southeast Asia, had a port call.

Friends had picked me up in San Fran, and took me to depart;
After having spent some time with others, to lighten
my questioning heart;
So off we drove in the back of a van, to get in another line;
To see weary faces, doubts for sure, and fear worn bravely
by some so fine.

Ranks ranged from private to colonel—across all services there;
Army, Navy, Marine Corps, and Air Force going off to where
All would serve our country, while striving to protect
our brothers;
A number older, many like me—some so young,
best left with their mothers.

I've not been to the slaughter pens, to see the cattle's last walk;
But for those of us there, standing in queue, 'twas ever so little talk;
If the cows had come to view us then;
had seen our path to that plane;
I know they would have looked forlorn—
would have understood our pain.

For if I had a film of those hours, spent at Travis
waiting to board;
Silence predominated, introspection, cutting enthusiasm
like a sword.
For the macho spirit of days just passed, around the country
in training camps;
Was traded for deafening silence, as we boarded slowly
up that ramp.

As I looked around that group of souls,
most were only focused ahead;
We moved as if like those cattle, some beginning to show the dread.
As our last foot raised off the ground to the metal, it hit us
each like lead;
That may be the last step in America, for some
would return quite dead.

I occasionally see that line today, give thought
to that roster of men;
Whose eyeballs seared, some dry, some damp—
squirming in seats when
The door closed shut, the seals in place,
on the TIA charter plane;
But we commenced to sit for three hours,
watching men sweat and strain.

The air conditioning unit had failed, as we were
by the crew, then told;
So we sat on that plane for an eternity, as to leave
surely some would fold.
Kept in our seats for several hours, till the
plane's systems checked ok;
The inevitable still ahead of us, might as well be
now on our way.

For we'd long since passed, the point: of what is called
diminishing return;
For some, indeed, to be exchanged—for the point
of no future yearn.
As I looked around, discerning, trying then to take it all in;
It hit me like a brick—that some arms, legs, eyeballs,
parts and bodies:
Would in the end not win!

Young men sent off to be slaughtered, along with the enemy, too;
But at least we were not as cattle, many
would fight to the death is true.
I've often wondered how many on that plane,
actually came back full of life;
For most I imagine they learned much, and
endured their share of strife.

For those who lived, most surely added: scar tissue,
imagined or real;
And for some the experience there, removed forever an even keel.
Certainly some who sat and stared back at me,
did not come back at all;
And you'll find their names now emblazoned—
deep in granite on The Wall.

Westward Across the Pond[1]

As we headed out across the pond;
It was a somber lot;
Faces pressed close to the windows;
For some returning, others not.

No laughter heard, let alone joy;
As we crossed the shoreline then;
On climbing out, our country's boys;
Hoping in twelve months, to see again.

The stewardesses in the cabin;
Making small talk as they went;
No alcohol served on these flights;
As America's sober prime was sent

Off to fight in a distant land;
Most drafted, and a few volunteers;
Late that afternoon, going to give a hand;
Wondering if we'd keep life dear.

The trip to Hawaii, for several hours;
Some got to know one another;
For me, was better then than most;
As I had with me three brothers.

---

[1]   Pilots have long referred to the Pacific Ocean as "the pond."

These FACs with whom I'd been through training;
Detwiler, Sifford, and Issaacson.
We passed the time with chatter;
Till the flight was over and done.

We arrived then in the land of fun;
Hawaii, in the dark of morn.
Around oh dark thirty, landing;
Most looked tired and so forlorn.

Into the airport's lounge at Hickam;
I recall still, the bar standing by;
Had a limit of one drink, was told;
So I ordered a tall mai tai.

The fuel trucks crawled up to the plane;
In the gloom of that weary morn;
Most wished the tanks would stay bone dry;
Or we somehow, would become reborn.

But then the call went out;
Announcing to board that plane.
Looking 'round the terminal;
Could quite easily see the pain.

Loaded up again, more talk now;
Than the previous day at Travis;
When we looked as if, but cows;
At other times sweet paradise, but for us antithesis.

And out we walked then, up the ramp;
And onto the cold, metal giant;
Whose engines turned, and fired up;
Flyers, Navy, the Corps and grunts.

Back in our seats, like all that war;
Had numbers, where we sat;
Most all of us, then lean, thought mean;
With but few then, wearing fat.

Took our seats, and taxied out;
The still quiet, soaking in;
Was dusk of morn, light showing through;
As we took off, once again.

Arrival

As the plane, then descended;

With the heat, closing in;

The white beaches of Cam Rahn;

Coasts of white, looking thin.

As we went through ten thousand;

Mountains looming so high;

And the green, all around there;

Will this be, where I die?

Two Good Men

Dedicated to Lts. Garrett E. Eddy, Rustic 23,
and Michael Stephen Vrablick
Killed in Action in the 0-2A They Were Flying
on October 1, 1970
In the Vicinity of Tang Kouk, Cambodia
The Wall: Panel 07W—Lines 103 and 104

On only one occasion, did we meet before their strife;
    But its amazing still today, how that memory lasts in life.
As a new guy in the 19th TASS[2], I'd just arrived at the hootch;
    Had no sooner met the unit's cat as well as "Lightning," the pooch.

When being introduced as a brown bar, it made for a real good laugh;
    But the shock of it all was the next day, I'd be reading their epitaphs.
Our unit's "primary" mission then, was that of flying the "CAP;"[3]
    Driving 'round the area, on some missions, might as well have napped.

Making sure that "rocket alley" did not come alive at night;
    So out of Saigon and Bien Hoa, the Viet Cong would not take a bite.
Thank goodness for small miracles, for 'twas introduced real soon:
    The "secondary," Top Secret mission, that to all was opportune.

For the landscape was so pock marked, with many hundreds of bombs;
    And darkness stretched from Tay Ninh City, all the way to
      Kompong Thom.

---

[2]   TASS = Tactical Air Support Squadron

[3]   CAP = Combat Air Patrol

It was our great fortune as young men, to work with these men so brave:
    Those Cambodians on the ground and the few in the air,
        were to us no knaves.

They fought with fearlessness, the likes of which I've never since once seen;
    Laid down an example of honor and duty, a shame for few have gleaned
The war fought in Cambodia, in Seventy through Seventy-Three
    May just as well have been fought on the moon, for few have
        yet come to see

Or hear of the exploits, the courage, the daring of these men from afar;
    But those Cambodians with whom we worked, most definitely
        raised the bar.
And that brings me back to the two young men, the day before just met:
    Garrett Eddy, the O-2 pilot, was determined not to let

The enemy make a fool of us, so he gave it all he had;
    Michael Stephen Vrablick, like most of us, was yet another lad
Who'd been there only a month or so, an O-1 driver he,
    But not short on enthusiasm, flew right seat with much glee.

Their mission on October First was convoy cover to Thom;
    To fly o'er head, scope out the road, and deliver trucks with calm
From Tang Kouk on up Highway 6, to lift the siege up there;
    To keep the bad guys' heads down—if required, give them a scare

By bringing fighters into play, dropping snake and nape, if needed;
    To deal the Khmer Rouge a blow, when their limits had been exceeded.
They left Bien Hoa way long before dawn, the convoy easily found;
    And started reconnoitering, seeking targets on the ground.

The clouds were low that weary day, broken to overcast;
    And what was even worse, that layer stayed low, right up until the last.
As only the Cambodians, and the Khmer Rouge, were those who
    were there;
        'Twas once room for speculation, but years later, two witnesses
        with care

Took me to the roadside thicket from which the machine guns fired;
    And then one farmer took us hence, to the field where the
    plane had become mired.
Undoubtedly Eddy found himself, in a situation not much envied:
    Do you sit on high and play it safe?—Or protect friends from
    the enemy?

One villager saw them cross the road, low, only a few clicks north;
    The problem was not that of only those clouds, but of luck—Yes!
                                                    Indeed a bad stroke.
For to go below those clouds, the plane: a silhouette it would become;
    Backlit by that thick layer of white—an easy prey that dawn for guns.

And as they flew from east to west, the .51 cals. sighted in;
    Convoy cover was easy on some days—not on this one to have been.
    As they approached the road, the machine guns, raised, loaded
    and took aim;
    And hit their mark, some Khmer Rouge gunner, so quickly
    gaining fame.

As the bullets tore at the aircraft, it looked as if stopped in midair;
    The villager, then but a boy of twelve, could see the gray metal tear.
Our plane staggered on across the road, only a few hundred feet above;
    Two men, if still alive then, fighting desperately to keep the
    life they loved.

But 'twas not to be that morning as their craft ran out of air;
    Crashing in front of a schoolhouse, they were destined to die
    as a pair
Of men who loved life as all of us do, fought for Freedom, Oh! So dear;
    Just as others who gave their all then, as now, so that we may
    today be here.

As the plane came then to rest, from Tang Kouk were soon dispatched
 A troop to recover their bodies—those lives that had just been snatched
In the crucible of war, these two had fought and given all they had.
 As the convoy stalled and made way for the troops, who passed
  by boiling mad;

Who headed for the crash site hurriedly, several kilometers northwest
 of town;
 They recovered them first, then sought out those who'd shot
  our pilots down.
Our aircrew lost to an act of war, two men met just yesterday;
 'Tis very sad, but true, this story, as war still has its way.

While Death is sad, but true enough, things sometimes but get worse;
 To think of it, and dwell on it, the truth was, oh, so ever terse:
 For one sorrowful aspect arose some months later, when to
  Vrablick a son was born;
A man who never saw his father, for his Dad was lost that morn.

While all on the ground there understood their plight, and all
 that came to pass;
 Was at first these circumstances unknown to us; as we were to
  find out last.
'Cause they'd given a position report only some brief time before;
 And the next plane then on station saw only a form on that
  jungle floor

Next to a rice field, near a pagoda, in front of the one room school;
 The aircrew saw that our friends below had arrived, to claim
  ours who'd lost that duel.
These are just two men who gave their lives, that others may prosper so;
 As the convoy proceeded to Kompong Thom, as others would
  also go.

Up that highway of Death in Nineteen and Seventy, Highway 6 as
     it was called;
     But got far worse before got better, as the war in Cambodia stalled.
We tend to forget as each year goes by, these men of long ago yesterday;
     They're but two of thousands who gave their lives for us,
          enough we cannot say.

For those who come visit in Washington, to The Wall, a stop they make;
     Please pay tribute to these two pilots who for us they gave their stake
In life that others may come and go, and do just as they please.
     Remember that good men and women, like these two, gave
          up a life of ease.

Our two pilots sacrificed their all that day, so that Freedom may
     always thrive;
     'Tis our duty now, our nation's, to keep their memories alive.
About Southeast Asia 'tis said today that: All Gave Some, while
     Some Gave All;
     So when you pass by look for these names: Eddy and Vrablick
          on The Wall.

The Saga of "Redeye" and "Sam"

In Honor of Robert N. Harris, Rustic 33—"Redeye"
and San Sok, Hotel 21—"Sam"

One of the pilots, in our group at Bien Hoa
    In March of Seventy One, while on a mission so far
From home base and out past, all our thin friendly lines
    He learned, for us all, a great lesson—one that'll stand for all time.

Takeoff was normal, on the one AM go;
    All systems checked out, most important fuel flow.
Artillery sectors en route, were checked with great care,
    For the last thing you'd want: meet a shell in midair.

Out the three thirteen radial, 'cross that invisible fence;
    Past Nui Ba Den, lonely sentinel—our last line of defense;
Into the unlit void of Cambodian jungle, immense rubber
    plantations, fields of rice;
    Would have loved to take others, on those "sightseeing" flights.

The weather was good, for a change that dark night;
    Our commute to work was but, a short forty-five minute flight.
One thing's for sure, there was never a rush hour
    As most in the world, would have thought our flights dour.

But to us as young men, with intentions to win;
    Press on to the ops area, cockpit lights going dim.
"Redeye" was in the left seat—pilot in command;
    Heading for the middle of Cambodia, and Khmer Rouge badland.

Just across the border; known to all as the "fence;"
    The darkness would envelope you, few lights going hence;
You might see a glow to the south, from Papa Papa, the city therein;
    To all the rest of the world, then as now, known as Phnom Penh;

Or Kompong Cham as most always, appeared on the nose—
    A serene beacon on the Mekong, a grand river of bows.
There was Kratie to the North, and next up Stoeng Treng,
    To go near either very low courted gunfire, losing lift from
      our wings;

'Cause you see that land 'round those towns, was to us quite unfriendly,
    Where head and shoulder could part; if caught on ground by
      the enemy.
'Course when a plane did go down, the war came to a halt;
    Airmen taking care of other airmen, could not be done to a fault.

So "Redeye," Rustic Three Three, flew over as on many nights before;
    Another young man, doing but his duty in war.
No fire fights that night, *T*roops *in* *C*ontact, known as TICs;
    So 'round the area, checking with ground commanders, only to see

If the enemy had harassed them, or our friends had intel to pass;
    So we could seek to hurt the bad guys, even better in mass.
One group on the ground, wanted light from the sky;
    So our pilot Bob Harris, dropped a flare going by.

Round three AM, "Redeye" changed course, and came upon Sam;
    "Hotel 21," his call sign—luck of the draw as it ran.
For most of the friendlies, with whom we worked on the ground;
    Were identified "Hotel," plus a number—an easily audible sound.

"Redeye" asked how it was—"all real quiet" said Sam that night;
    And he began conversation, to "Redeye's" delight.
Sam talked of his once teaching, math in high school;
    Manning radios now, in that dark morass below—Sam was no fool.

He was in for the fight of his life, you could see;
    The sound of his voice, belied the true gravity.
The Air Force had its orders, from some folks then on high—
    Top Secret was the mission, which was most highly classified.

For by all rights as pilots, we were not there at all—
    Certainly not in Cambodia, not supporting Lon Nol.
Responding to calls when the enemy pressed, thick battle in gear;
    Or just passing the time—"holding hands" in the "clear;"

For our friends on the ground—a disheveled tired lot;
    A single goal 'mongst them all—gain freedom, or die by gunshot.
They were giving their lives, we had seen many times;
    Not to come to their aid, would have been the real crime.

So "Redeye" was there, on that night distant past
    To give relief, boost morale, help run the hour glass
To the daylight of morn, when some fear could be shed
    By our friends on the ground, those dark nights they so dread.

As talk went along then—Sam said: "indebted am I"—
    As but just a forlorn foot soldier, then talking to "Redeye":
A debt that he stated, he could never repay to those, who assisted
    him in his hard fight;
    That message made a young pilot's job, much easier that long night.

Wasn't patronizing or clever, just a man from his heart;
    That brought our work to the forefront, as Sam struggled to impart:
All Sam said he wanted, was to Live Free or Die—
    Seems folks from New Hampshire, have heard just that cry.

'Twas a shame that radio call, could not 'round the world go;
    But for "Redeye" that night, the real meaning cleared so
As to put all into focus, our job simple and small:
    On the one hand we'd give support, so our friends like Sam
        wouldn't fall;

On the other much grander, if all did their part:
    Freedom would take hold, in a new world with a start.
Deep within Cambodia, on that hot humid night
        'Twas prophetic that a radio transmission, so brief, yet so bright;

Would mirror cries for help, that have been heard 'round the world;
    That has led our country into battle, with our flags all unfurled.
Sam's statements that night, put it so in perspective;
    For all of us who love freedom, we should forever be reflective:

That when we as a nation, extend a helping hand for freedom to reign—
    Most important of all, we should finish what's started—Yes!—
        Stay and sustain.
'Twas not the case in Southeast Asia, as all came to see;
    For that war, so confusing to many, but not so to we

Who flew there 'midst joys, and sorrows so strong;
    Only wish we could have stayed there, till right was made
        from wrong.
But "Redeye" that night from Sam: a valuable lesson we gained;
    That made our work, with such fine brethren, all the more sane.

Unfortunately that fulfillment—Freedom—was not to be then;
    But "Redeye's" shared this message, with many since when
Sam manned the radio, on Highway 6 in Tang Kouk;
    And "Redeye," but a lieutenant, with whom Sam then spoke.

I only wish all the world, could have been there that night,
    Along with "Redeye" in that cockpit, on another of America's
        liberty flights.
If just more would have heard, or now hear, Sam's words so charged
    and so clear;
        Perhaps more 'mongst us now, would hold our freedom most dear.

My Peashooter

As pilots in Southeast Asia, we wore survival vests;
    With radios, batteries, food and signals, maps to make us best.
For a weapon we were given, a thirty-eight caliber gun;
    A Smith and Wesson Combat Masterpiece, but better learn to run.

For such a small pistol lacked power, loaded full, with only six
    small rounds.
    My plan was to start running, before I hit the ground!
If I had to bail out—hit the silk, or make a landing forced;
    I thought I'd better run and hide, the better plan to live, of course.

For my mighty little thirty-eight, did not pack such a punch;
    Might be ok for an enemy or two, but certainly not a bunch.
Or maybe as in Alaska, when you're chased by a grizzly bear;
    Best to use five shots on the beast of fur, then put one in your ear.

Would have made more trouble than it was worth, far more than it
    could handle;
    When alighting on the ground, running from those who wore
        those sandals;
If that had happened, indeed, would have been hard, to see the
    glass half full;
    'Cause I certainly would not have been stopping, to sit and
        shoot the bull.

But that's the story of our little pistol, small black six shot gun;
    I did not want to meet my foes with it, 'cause it would not
        have been much fun.
Is like too many things in life: is easier to get into than out of.
    So if I had any choice at all, I'd stay the ground, above.

I would have been willing to have flown my plane, damaged and
    full of holes;
    In hopes of saving for tomorrow my bacon, my body, and my soul.
But better than nothing, that's for sure, it gave some peace of
    mind;
    But had I landed on the ground, I did not want to find

The men that I'd been looking for, almost every day.
    Don't think my little thirty-eight, would have held them much
        at bay.
But after all it was my peashooter, not great, but better than a knife;
    I sure am glad, however, that it didn't have to save my life.

Spelunking O'er Cambodia

Dedicated to the Night Rustics and to the
Men Who Manned the Radios—Our Lifeline—
at Rustic Alpha on Nui Ba Den

And vertigo beckoned, in the luminescent glare;
Of the swaying light, of the glistening flare;
As the chute came opened, and brightened the night;
Making night into day, for the oncoming fight.

What was called candlepower, was a bit overstated;
But that light in the cave, was certainly first rated;
'Cause the cave's dimensions, could better be seen;
And the enemy there, could be best then gleaned.

That's how it was, when at the end of your tether;
The radio's lifeline, like a rope in a cave;
In the midst of Cambodia, a world rather nether;
For pilots so young, but not long then babes.

'Twas long years ago, happened surely it did;
But so few were aware; 'fore the story was hid;
Kept from the public, while good men there died;
And the bodies were buried, as those in power but lied.

Wish they could have traveled, down those paths in that cave
Been in the cockpit, as we tried once to save
Men who fought valiantly, there died for their cause;
One we had promised, was worthy of pause.

For freedom they spoke of, on the radios then;
They looked to America, for power to win.
And while working and fighting, searching deep in that cave;
In our desire to find right, so little we gave.

America then lost, a small piece of itself;
O'er the jungles and rice fields, scant of much wealth.
Had the folks back home heard, those voices below;
They would have harked better, the fighting to sow.

But the cost of it all, was hidden from view;
Cause protesters gathered, voices, more than few
Wanted war then to end, to back out of the cave;
So we stopped our spelunking, and arrested the wave.

Of troops that had gone, many lost to the East;
Tens of thousands and more, but far from the least;
As others back home, had nephews, brothers and sons;
Those gone all too soon, 'cause of bullets and guns.

But when casting back then, to recall bygone flights;
Those hours spent spelunking, on long ago nights;
Deep in the cave of Cambodia's walls;
Down deep, distant routes, of rich jungled halls.

Through the thick air, tempered, black with few lights;
Only twinkling, yellow sparkles, red tracers' delight;
A few campfires burning, occasional rice field on fire;
Our friends' plight below, so often quite dire.

As they surely gave depth, to our passage of flight;
Brought dimension to why, we were there but to fight.
It was thrilling to work with men, oh, so brave;
Those ones down below, at the base of that cave.

And sorrowful it was, that so many then gave
Of their families, their lives, so little to rave.
And if only folks now, would envision that cave;
Where freedom was sought, by so many back then;

Perhaps understand better why some, all they gave;
And why others gave some, with no chance to win.
It's the effort 'twas made, that's what it's about
Not only just winning, when having the clout.

For those flights in that cave, with its walls wet and stark;
It was freedom back then, that shined in the dark.
The men that died there, both our friends and below;
Left their marks on the walls, of that cave with a glow.

'Twas an honor to enter, those cave's halls of night;
To fight with good men, midst the glare of the light;
When those flares burst forth, illuminating sky;
And the ground just beneath, as the fighters flew by.

No lights from our planes, for good targets would make;
Just fleeting shadows, as the ground then would shake;
From the bombs dropped with care, accuracy prevailed;
Midst the gunfire directed skyward, such red burning hail.

As the napalm's fires stretched, o'er targets just beneath;
'Twas good to fight then, for our rights and beliefs.
No matter what was, said back then, or even now;
Am glad we saw action in that cave, none did cow.

As men, the Night Rustics, crawled down in that cave;
With others just like us, to fight and to save.
Those nights once we left, the lights of Tay Ninh;
At the door of the cave, as we entered to win.

Could only but hope, as we passed Nui Ba Den;
Looked out at our lifeline, our friends that were kin.
Crawled slowly across, that dense growth below;
Looked so bleak, pitch black, with nothing aglow.

As we crept slowly westward, t'ward the Mekong we flew;
On those lonely bygone nights, a crew of but two;
Along those walls of the cave; at times, damp as any could be;
Looking keenly below, while hoping to see

Trucks on the roads, troops in movement below;
Supplies on those sampans, our enemy on the go;
Was thrilling to be there, in the thrall of that chamber;
As kilometers passed, with coordinates sought.

And stumble upon, some fine lines with bright camber;
Those arches of tracers; with gunners distraught;
For when they missed, as was thankfully, often the case;
Followed back to the source, at the light's downward base.

'Twas for those Khmer Rouge, who crawled along on that floor;
When their hand in the dark, they would at times, boldly show;
Would make the night come alive, fast the time it would fly;
As the planes, they would circle, as others would die.

And that was the story, of spelunking in the past;
As we would back east head, at times but aghast;
To our door and the bright, sun shining, through the prop;
Back through the cave, yet another combat hop.

'Twas spelunking at its best, and thrilling it was;
On occasion to drop down, in darkness and buzz;
The floors of that cave, that could come quickly alive;
Wish that only those we'd fought with, had come since to thrive.

But few whom we worked with, came to survive;
As all too many, then gave of their lives;
And for the few who lived then, so many were stopped;
By the reign of terror, that was then of Pol Pot.

And one may but wonder, had we stayed there to win;
Yes, we'd have lost, some more of our kin;
But the pain of it all, would not be as great;
Had the Khmer Republic, had a chance for its fate.

Just like in sports, when the trade off is seen;
For short term pain, may be realized the more;
Long term gain, the result may redeem;
And once and forever, even the score.

Moonlight on the Mekong

For my fellow Night Rustics, those men with whom I flew in
combat over Cambodia on those nights of long ago years.

As you come upon the Mekong;
When flying late at night;
The shimmering streaks of moonbeams;
A luminescent sight.

From Stoeng Treng south to Kratie;
'Tis like a string or pearls;
'Round Southeast Asia's stunning neck;
It's eddies, some aswirl.

Runs west, to the Prek Kak Plantation;
Widening, as it flows along;
And when it turns, to south again;
The currents, getting strong.

Passes by the town of Kompong Cham;
A haven once for us;
A friendly town, a beacon there;
A welcome sight 'twas thus.

For there in mid Cambodia;
The lights shown every night;
And as we arrived, on station;
Was such a welcome sight.

Then turned the river, west again;
On its way, down to the sea;
Meandering back and forth a bit;
As the moonlight skipped with glee.

For as you saw the river;
The moonbeams danced like spikes;
Along the ripples of its passage;
As millions of white shining knights.

Was grand to see that stream when lit;
Could make out men and boats;
For when the moon shone down quite bright;
Freed darkness from its coat.

And that was kind, liked all the more;
To make out motion better then;
To use the river and the moon;
As tools of war, away back when.

And as the water trickled on;
Past Phnom Penh, as it clung;
With its muddy froth, infused with silt;
Back to the east by south, it swung.

On its swaying path, through the delta;
Passing carcasses, and metal hulks below;
Of ships blown high, en route to town;
With explosives, gave the horizon such a glow.

Such a fine, and beautiful lady;
Not young, or thin and sleek;
But slow and lazy, looked from above;
But not for swimming, by the meek.

And lastly passing Tan Chou,
Where convoys once departed;
Ran the gauntlet north through rocket alley;
Up to Phnom Penh, where the war was charted.

But on a quiet night, in heat seared sky;
'Twas a brilliance to behold;
Not built for speed, but comfort;
Glistening radiance, for one so old.

As the moonlight's ripples sparkled;
Was hard at times to grasp;
That some men would die in the Mekong's hold;
And be there, forever clasp.

For as young men, who flew over;
That mighty thread, reflecting bright;
On those moonlit nights of long ago;
But few are to her equal, as an inspiring sight.

So old is not all bad, you see;
'Cause the Mekong will be there;
When our wars are long forgotten;
She'll still pass along with care.

But moonlight on the Mekong;
Is a sight most will recall;
Had they been there once, to take it in;
Flickering beams, at that great dance hall.

Such a wondrous show of lights;
Glowing through the fog of war;
If only we could rid ourselves;
Of battles fought, forever more;

Then folks could take their children;
To see that cavorting light;
On the Mekong's dazzling surface;
On some distant future night.

The Interpreters

Dedicated to the OV-10 backseaters, all volunteers, who used their fluency of French to assist our Cambodian allies, and especially Gil Bellefeuille, Ron Dandeneau, Walt Friedhofen, Roger Hamann, Marcel Morneau and Joe Paquin, all of whom waited over 30 years to each receive the awards of the Distinguished Flying Cross they so greatly deserved and to Ron Gamache, Phil Morneault and Joe Vaillancourt who likewise waited over 30 years to receive their aircrew wings.

Theirs is a story that needs to be told;
For they were indeed, a great part of the fold;
They were all volunteers, who spoke fluent French;
To assist our great allies, when found in a pinch.

Some were clerks, but brave, not trained then for war;
But they rallied with such spirit, for what was in store.
They flew o'er Cambodia, and helped save lives then;
As Rustic Airborne Interpreters, away back when.

Some were typing one day, and in flight suits the next;
But rapidly they learned, as if they'd had the best text;
Their job was noble, helping men on the ground;
These men came to love, the grand work they had found.

'Cause excitement was there, when called into battle;
Fighting the Khmer Rouge, who treated people like chattel;
It was easy you see, to fly missions so far;
Into the heart of Cambodia, to help others some more.

These men, they flew missions, of four hours or so;
To take to the enemy, our fiercest of blows;
Courageous, heroic, yes, gallant, one and all;
Regardless of outcome, they will always stand tall.

'Cause they gave it their best, and saved many a life;
Reduced many times, for our friends, their worst strife;
They worked with our allies, on the ground down below;
And gave them much hope, when they suffered such blows.

They beat back the enemy, with fighters and gunships;
And saved a few pilots, as Death tried on its grip;
They watched for the tracers, the gunfire around;
For the antiaircraft thick, at times did abound.

It was not so unusual, to man five radios then;
No doubt they'd worked more, had it helped them to win;
And true to their mettle, with nerves as of steel;
They, with their pilots, would turn aircraft on heel.

The OV-10 Bronco, was quite a wonderful sight;
For Cambodians on the ground, it approached sheer delight;
To see those twin props, as they sliced through the air;
Bringing hope to our friends, that the world would be fair.

They rolled and they looked, for the enemy there;
Flew o'er the Mekong, peering down with honed care;
T'ward that river of old, through Cambodia it flowed;
Looking out for the sampans and Khmer Rouge, our foes.

They saved many a man, used their language and skills;
While having for them, some of life's greatest thrills.
You can't do much more, than strive to save lives;
And in that long ago job, those men surely thrived.

These interpreters worked, many days in a row;
To make the world better, at least a bit so;
They braved monsoons and thunder, lightning and lead;
On a classified mission, most far from their beds.

Was nothing to travel, a hundred miles or more;
To support our fine allies, help even the score.
And sad is the story, for so many did give;
But only few of our brethren, survived the battles to live.

But the story now told, is of men who gave all;
Of their energy, their drive, with the mission enthralled;
Can be said of these men, only known to but few;
Gave then, more than most, while few Americans knew.

But the story of these men, can be told now today;
Of their boldness, their fearless, and exceptional way.
'Twas my great privilege, to have known a few then;
And the world's far better, for having these men.

A Water Buffalo Has the Last Laugh

As so often happens in war, animals bear the brunt of conflict.

One late afternoon, while flying low, over the wide Mekong;
    Near the Prek Kak Plantation—river running, lazily along;
A gunship checked in with me, and having no targets in sight;
    So I chatted with him awhile, before dusk turned to night.

And then as I saw him, flying above me, over the radio he said
    Into his mike, he had a target—one suitable for lead.
Down below I saw little, and nothing of much consequence:
    Rubber trees in the plantation, and jungle, really dense.

On the river, 'twas no traffic, just a water buffalo, there bathing—
    And much to my dismay, that's the target he was craving.
Unfortunately the gunship, needed then no clearance from me;
    So he took aim, as I stood clear, and he fired with so much glee.

To be sure, some would argue, that the beast there, down below;
    Had probably carried rockets, and ammunition for our foe.
But as often happens in war, as many who fight do find—
    They're frequently kinder to animals, than to some humankind.

Not for the pilot of the gunship, as he turned on his firepower;
    Perhaps creating for our beast—just a much needed shower.
As the water around that animal rose, like a geyser, ever high;
    Those seven point six-two machine guns, kept firing from the sky.

When the weapons ceased their fusillade, and the water settled down;
>   Then out of the river, marched the bulky brute—waddling
>   like a clown.
I next flew down to see him, and made a real low pass.
>   Don't think those rounds scored at all—as he just sauntered
>   t'ward the grass.

When secure up on the shore, the beast looking fit as a fiddle;
>   He glanced up at me as if 'twas hurt—not a bit, not even a little.
The last I saw of that water buffalo, moving sluggishly below;
>   Was as he tromped down a path of grass, with a grin—and leering so!

As I saw that beast of burden, from my viewpoint, very near;
>   It was such a wonderful feeling—I thought that I would cheer.
And for those today who read this, and may take quite some
offense—
>   'Twas an isolated incident, and in the end—Of no consequence!

Missing One Fin

When flying the Cessna 02-A in combat the normal ordnance upload for daytime missions was two pods of 2.75" white phosphorous, or "willie pete," rockets as they were usually called. Each of these pods contained seven *folding fin artillery rockets* (FFARs). On night missions, only one pod was carried on a weapons station beneath the wing that then allowed for the other three ordnance stations to be used for four flares and two log markers.

The target would be sighted through the gunsight and care would be given as to managing your altitude, dive angle and airspeed in order to obtain optimum results. Once the trigger was engaged in the cockpit, the rocket's engine would ignite and the rocket would exit the pod or tube. Each of four fins attached at its base were designed to unfold simultaneously to provide stability in flight and to assist in accuracy in hitting the target. Needless to say, when these fins did not operate as designed, the rocket lost all semblance of having a planned trajectory. In such instances the rocket became dangerous to all, both on the ground and in the air.

When exiting the tube a bright exhaust plume from the rear of the rocket could be seen. This, while quite apparent, was of little consequence in the daytime. However, at night the pilot sighted the target through a dimmed reticle in the non-computing gunsight directly in front of him at eye level. He would take care to avoid looking at the rocket as it exited the tube.

If he caught the bright plume in his line of sight, or to an extent in his periphery, while the rocket was in close proximity to the airplane, it would destroy the pilot's night vision for a brief period of time. This would then contribute to the increased likelihood of spacial disorientation, given the high degree of maneuvering that would immediately precede and follow the firing of the marking rocket. Vertigo at night, along with weather, ground fire, jinking to avoid becoming a more stationary target, and maintaining a knowledge of your position deep over the middle of Cambodia, made for an interesting mission to say the least.

Firing folding fin rockets, were the weapon of choice;
    When marking targets for fighters—most FACs would rejoice.
But on occasion when firing, the rocket leaving the pod;
    A folding fin would not open—creating sights, thus quite odd.

The rocket's trajectory, wandering all over the sky;
    Heading for the ground, then toward space it would fly.
Would look like a missile—gone ballistic for sure;
    And would end up down range—providing no cure

For the fighters to sight, on the target below.
    But at night when it happened—Was quite a bright show!
Nothing accomplished, when one went thus awry;
    A wonder to behold, as it flew erratically high.

And then a mark distant, would appear on the ground;
    A few klicks from the target, when the earth it had found.
Such are the spectacles, of weapons designed to prevail.
    Most get the job done, but on occasion some fail.

The Log Marker—What a Weapon!

Dedicated to Bill Lemke, Rustic 27, who from several thousand feet above the target, perfected a vertical dive at night heading directly toward the ground. This achieved a high degree of accuracy and resulted in placing the log marker where desired. In effect, the issues of dive angle, airspeed and altitude for release were greatly minimized and the effects of wind on the weapon when delivered in this manner were diminished. It was quite a delivery to experience at night based on comments from those who flew in his right seat. But like many innovations in combat, it got the job done. My delivery was usually far less accurate and, hence, my distaste for the log marker.

As a pilot in the 0-2, we carried weapons on our wings;
    Rocket pods and flares, plus a strange looking thing.
Those makers of weapons, so smug and so bright;
    Created the log marker, dropped on the ground to give light.

We'd fly over a target, like a bomber above;
    Take a wag on the wind, therein lies part of the rub.
We'd then hit the "drop" switch—it would parachute down;
    Providing a beacon for us all, as it sat on the ground.

'Course one thing we lacked, in Cambodia at night
    Was a weather station, that on winds, could shed decent light.
Perhaps the rice fields below, when the farmers were burning;
    That might help us determine, which way winds were turning.

But from two thousand feet, or so, up on high;
    As we flew straight and level, dropping the log, with a sigh;
'Cause this exercise, gave new meaning, to wild ass guess;
    When hitting the release switch—would cause some distress.

I felt, as if flying, one of those great biplanes of old;
    Releasing grenades from my hands, that I would but hold;
Might as well, have been World War One, flying a Jenny;
    As dropping the log marker, with variables so many.

But we went off to fight, with one more munition;
    To throw at the enemy—To get his attention!
I'd not had much luck, with the few that I'd dropped;
    'Cause you had no control, of how the parachute popped.

So with altitude, airspeed, wind and elevation of the mark;
    The log's light went downward, in the night, as if on a lark.
One thing's for certain, when all's said and done;
    Thanks to gravity alone—it hit the ground—if targets, but none.

Then one night, during the fierce Battle of Prey Totung;
    A log marker out on my wing, from which it was slung.
If all went well, it would drop to the ground;
    Providing a bright beacon, for those fighters inbound.

We flew o'er the area, my right seater working hard;
    His window open, our lights out, and definitely on guard.
For we'd taken fire, from several machine gun sites;
    And didn't relish flying, straight and level that night.

As we approached the point, that we'd agreed would be best;
    My right seater looking down, gave corrections for our quest.
He called "drop" and my finger, hit the switch as before;
    Dropping that log marker, assuredly, my least favorite store.

We then began to jink abruptly, changing altitude and turning;
As we waited for our log marker, to hit the ground and start burning.
I'll never forget that moment, of enthusiastic surprise;
For our marker lit bright, exactly where we'd aimed—as if
we'd won a prize!

The beleaguered commander, on the ground was delighted;
And fortunately the fighters, keyed mikes as they sighted
Our bright beacon, right on target, unbelievably so;
But to our dismay, as the battle then unfolded below:

Those engineers of weapons, had most likely forgot—
That among the enemy's arsenal, was the shovel, and apparently lots.
'Cause as we flew over, and began controlling, the first airstrike;
Our log marker began dimming, as if nothing but a rheostat light.

The commander below, while taking fire from all around;
Said the Khmer Rouge were shoveling dirt, on our marker they'd found.
Throwing earth on our beacon, so much effort that night;
We'd given to our target marker, but not giving thought slight

To the fact that our enemy, ingenious and bold;
Would merely scoop soil on our light, making it grow so cold.
'Course one thing was obvious, for all who were there;
The enemy was near our marker, and showing little care.

Then only one thing to do, as the light grew but dimmer;
Put a bomb on our marker, so the enemy's ranks would be thinner.
This we accomplished promptly, to the commander's joy;
Guess our marker served its purpose, much as a decoy.

The commander on the ground, additionally that night;
Said the light from our marker, had put a few in his sights.
So as weapons, we used on those long ago nights;
I'd rate the marker not useless, but somewhat lacking in firefights.

I hope it helped others, but in my experience: little except that night;
    Was accomplished with that weapon—no matter how bright.
So all was not lost, on that night, as we came to agree;
    But I'd rather use flares and rockets, for the fighters to see.

There was yet an additional cause, for pilots' concern;
    For as lights and campfires, on the ground would but burn
On those dark nights that were murky, from rice fields afire;
    And sometimes on such nights, that were but a quagmire;

Those lights on the ground, might be mistaken for stars;
    Adding to the spacial disorientation, that could only but mar;
When you went to make a pass, to shoot a rocket as a lance;
    It was far wiser to trust instruments, than seat of the pants.

So our log marker helped those, on the ground that bleak night;
    And with luck on our side, took a few bad guys from the fight.
It's the only time, I ever recall, that weapon unique helping us out;
    But then after all, on that dark night, for us it had some real clout.

Arc Light

One night out in the AO[4], I'd failed to get the radio call;
    That en route to a target near, were B-52's, loaded wall to wall.
They carried one hundred eight—five hundred pounders, as I recall
        the count;
And if the enemy was in their zone, his losses were soon to mount.

A call went out on guard—my attention was promptly obtained;
    Turned tail out of the area—'cause I wanted my life retained.
The first I saw behind me, was an ever growing glow;
    And then the concussion hit, as my plane was all too slow.

Buffeted about like a toy, that was thrown around by hand;
    I then turned to see the spectacle—bright, explosive and
        exceptionally grand.
The strings of bombs were walking, across the nocturnal landscape near;
    Maybe at most six or seven klicks—barely out of range, and clear.

After witnessing the strike called Arc Light—fireworks today look small;
    With bombs exploding, seemed everywhere—such multitudinous
        fireballs.
The light from all the ordnance, appeared to turn night into day;
    Don't see how anyone in those bombs' path—could have
        gotten clean away.

---

[4]   AO = Area of Operations

I heard of the mass of destruction, on occasion when our choppers flew in;
    Just after the debris settled to the ground, with our enemies'
        heads in a spin.
If the bombs did not succeed in killing or maiming, those found
    were simply numb;
        For if they lived, the least damage of all, was the rupturing of
        their ear drums.

And today when in Cambodia, you can still see the Arc Lights' scale;
    Each flights' sticks of bombs' craters, having once created bleak
        and dismal trails.
So if these flights of bombers—perhaps sometimes, not the enemy hurt;
    Then made plenty of bamboo toothpicks, and moved a lot of dirt.

The Cobra and the Mongoose

While on my combat tour, in that far off, distant place;
    Many bought statues, others just happy with fine lace.
On a planned mission o'er Cambodia, to be diverted to Thailand;
    My senior, clever, crew chief, had contrived a dubious plan.

He wanted a stuffed mongoose, and cobra in a fight;
    Mongoose lunging upward, the cobra poised to strike.
I thought but nothing of it, as I headed for my plane;
    With map cases, scope, binoculars, and not much then inane.

Pre-flight, taxi, takeoff, climb out, cruise t'ward the west;
    Time for the nightly show, time to give it all our best.
Flew the mission then, next headed, northward for Ubon;
    Certainly beat heading easterly, back into that bright lit sun.

Debriefed then after landing, taking the last baht bus to town;
    Got into civvies, had a meal, with a few cold brews to drown.
Had many things to pick up, for the guys back at Bien Hoa;
    Thailand's 'most like heaven, just like landing in a spa.

Gathered boots at Dan Thong's, at Maharaja's: fitted clothes;
    Then on to the jewelry shop, for princess rings in droves.
And last, but not the least—that cobra and mongoose to go;
    Wish that I could lose them both; viewed that pair as foes.

Out to the aircraft at dusk, to pre-flight, load it up so high;
    It was filled with all too much, for to jump up in the sky.
We rolled, and then we rolled some more, nursed it off the ground;
    Like a tanker full of gas, seeking all the lift that could be found.

In the back, I'd strapped the stuff down, so none would shift on
    that flight;
      'Cause there were storms to fly around, before getting home
        that night.
The mission demanded full attention, so then occupied, I became;
      Working with our friends on the ground, the storm throwing
        buckets of rain.

With fuel now dwindling down, and my relief bird on his way;
    I turned southeast, leaned both engines, thinking only of my hay.
The turbulence got worse then, with lightning strikes in bolts;
      My plane quite small bounced-up, down and sideways—as if
        just a colt.

Tightening my seatbelt, and then yet tighter, as the ride was no more fun;
      The rain poured on, and the wind it swirled—would be glad
        when I was done.
'Twas dark outside, but for the lightning, cockpit lights on low;
      When on the back of my bare neck, I felt a tapping, then, just so!

My instant reaction was to turn around—what was that to my rear?
      But two beady eyes, forked tongue and fangs, and a hood that
        struck:
                              With fear!
The cobra and the mongoose, had broken loose, trying to claim
    yet one more life;
      With a rush of shock and adrenaline, my brain sensed worse,
        than a knife!

If my plane had only come like some, equipped with an ejection seat;
      The handles raised, I would have departed, for the jungle
        would have beat.
Just seated there and helpless, my thirty-eight quite useless then;
      Can't remember to this day, ever pumping more adrenaline,
        since when.

But as the seat was bolted down, and those binding straps were tight;
　For anyone that could have seen, must have been a frightful sight!
The position in which I found myself, I'd been out of there for sure;
　As those seconds, then in passing, seemed liked years as I endured.

The realization that I was still alive, came as sweat poured down my face;
　And I lost more than a few heartbeats, as my pump was in a race.
It's unbelievable how fast your body, responding to fear brought
　on so fast;
　　I thought that moment, still frozen in time, was to surely
　　have been my last.

But as I managed to settle down a bit, and calm myself more then;
　There'd been no question as to fight or flight—if those fangs
　had but sunk in.
For my efforts to depart the plane, as the straps had taken hold;
　Leaving bruises to show, later laughed at, my thoughts not
　very bold.

As I settled more and turned around, then to strap the cobra down;
　The storm abated, light shown from the east, and I felt more
　like a clown.
For foolishly placing those stuffed pests, on top of the things I'd
　brought back;
　　I'd paid dearly for that error, and for the intelligence that a
　　lieutenant lacked.

After landing, elated that my mission was done, but even more
　next, when I stood;
　　I took to my crew chief, those two fierce animals, still mounted
　　so on wood.
Was grand to walk from that cockpit, and to myself keep within,
　my case of fear;
　　To have lived on just another day there, with that hooded
　　cobra, oh, so near.

I could only surmise what might have been, had the critter but been alive;
    Would have ruined my day for sure, quite unable to have been revived;
But even stuffed, had those fangs sunk into my neck, I'd been just as dead;
    As if there'd been venom in that snake, or my plane had been
      full of lead.

Fire Support Base Blue

Dedicated to the men who fought that night, February 23, 1971,
at Fire Support Base Blue, III Corps, Republic of Vietnam—to
those Killed in Action and Wounded in Action—and to the two
Rustic Forward Air Controllers who were on station and saved
lives, then First Lieutenants James M. Gibbar, Rustic 25, and
Robert N. Harris, Rustic 33. On December 10, 2002, the
United States Air Force issued Directives awarding the
Distinguished Flying Cross to both Col. James M. Gibbar,
USAFR (Retired), and Mr. Robert N. Harris—
recognition well deserved and long overdue.

One night in nineteen seventy-one,
23rd of February, 'twas then;
The enemy lay crouching, ready—
To attack our American men.

Was at the far reaches of Three Corps;
Just 'fore you cross the Fence.
That imaginary border 'tween Cambodia
And South Vietnam, from whence:

The Rustics flew, to aid the Khmers;
Throughout day, and into night.
To stem the tide of tyranny;
Take to them, the might of right.

And as the story unfolds, that eve;
The men out on the line;
Were sitting down, enjoying life;
As best they could, not fine.

The jungle came up near the base;
Blue, was its name back then;
Artillery, for Fire Support;
Creating noise, made quite a din.

And in the darkness, way out west;
A sentinel, returning to base;
Came upon the start of battle;
Saving lives, was then the race.

And as the craft took over;
Coordinating help;
A call went out, for another ship;
So that more force could be dealt.

The plane launched from alert, that night;
It's rockets, flares uploaded;
To wade into the battle then;
Not needing to be goaded.

For the job of the FACs, on board;
Was to bring the fight, close in;
Take to the enemy, our very best;
That we had from American men.

The call went out for fighters;
The attack aircraft, rolled in;
Then down the chute, delivering;
One pass, and then again.

The next round brought a gunship;
The FACs controlled that night;
And it, too, took its surest aim;
So as to win this fight.

And on the ground was agony,
As men fell, one by one,
The shots rang out, the calls and yells;
As the base, was overrun.

The FACs above, worked busily;
Manning radios and weapons then;
In hopes of saving lives and limbs;
In that early dawn, to win.

The next act in the scene of war;
The medevacs to come;
Those Dustoff choppers, bringing hope;
For lives and limbs, just some.

The FACs stood steady, facing fire;
And in the end, prevailed;
They'd delivered flares and strength;
With the battle, now curtailed.

They helped save, twenty-three wounded there;
Our men who took much fire;
And gave our foes that night, back then;
Consequences, yes, quite dire.

The FACs came back to base, that night;
They had served, that others might;
Live to see, again, another day;
To live, and, if needed, fight.

These men were fine Americans;
From where many have been born;
But from our country's womb, that night;
Five others, were but torn.

Those five who gave their lives at Blue;
So that buddies, and comrades all;
Would but think of their great sacrifice;
When now visiting The Wall.

Shot Down

Dedicated to Lts. Garrett E. Eddy, Rustic 23,
and Michael Stephen Vrablick
Killed in Action in the 0-2A They Were Flying
on October 1, 1970
In the Vicinity of Tang Kouk, Cambodia
The Wall: Panel 07W—Lines 103 and 104

O'er the rice fields of Cambodia
Only doing jobs.
In the middle of that country;
Young lives quickly robbed.

Helping to gain Freedom
For men they did not know;
Risking lives for others then
For Liberty—to sow.

So the world may be a better place,
They laid down life and limb.
May be said of all who died there;
With numbers; oh, so grim!

The two young souls, that morning
Did not know it was their last.
Young vibrant men with purpose;
Life wrenched from both so fast.

You can only sit and wonder;
Today we have when, where and how.
But even though we know the answer;
Can't help but ask why, even now.

Lunch, Anyone?

Dedicated to the Army helicopter scouts, many of whom were young warrant officers (WO). All of them gave courage a new meaning. And specifically to the two men, whose identities remain unknown to me, who died when their OH-6 went down in our Area of Operations, in December, 1970, in the Cambodian jungle approximately 27 miles east of Kompong Cham, Cambodia.

On March 22, 1999, I stood at the location of their crash site in the middle of Cambodia with members of the Joint Task Force team who were working there to recover remains. As I viewed what appeared to be an archaeological site, it was difficult to envision the agony of that crew's last minutes of life as their chopper crashed and burned, their lives lost in the forsaken jungle of Southeast Asia far away from friends and family.

The young Army scouts were appropriately matched to the OH-6 or light observation helicopter. Both were feisty and full of energy. The bird was generally referred to as a "loach." This was once explained to me as having been derived from "LOCH" for *l*ight *o*bservation *ch*opper or "LOH" for *l*ight *o*bservation *h*elicopter. Regardless, when you saw one working, it was truly something to behold. And as the poem relates, the young scouts kept everyone on their toes.

One bright sunny day, as I worked across the fence;
   Working with an Army pink team, o'er the jungle, oh, so dense;
A *c*ommand *and c*ontrol chopper—"C and C"—flying up above;
   A Cobra gunship at the ready—for the enemy, had no love.

And down below at treetop height, was a chopper with a bubble;
   A young Army warrant officer, hanging it out, looking hard for trouble.

The "pink team" was a combination, of the choppers working like glue,
    Zigging and zagging every which way, using tactics that proved
        so true.

The WO in the OH-6, or loach, as it was called;
    Would hover over jungle canopy, seeking the enemy to scald.
He'd part the tops of trees, with blasts of downward air;
    From the Loach's blades above, while showing little care.

For himself, he was to all, little more than bait;
    As the rest of us stood at the ready, not much to do but wait.
The Loach would dart here and there, seeking bunkers to attack;
    And when he found, the Cobra'd roll in, firing rockets off his rack.

And if the enemy showed himself, then I was there to call;
    Fighter bombers to launch airstrikes, leaving thick black
        smoke—a pall.
But as the Loach moved in and out, of the jungle treetops there;
    I sensed he had then on his mind, something else for which
        he cared.

And sure enough when the chopper, crossed a tree line just below;
    He saw a hootch, a nice wide yard, and settled down just so.
The C & C ship called to see, just what the young man then had found;
    No answer for us up above, as he prepared to exit on the ground.

I dropped in lower to the west, the Cobra gunship to the east;
    It took not long to figure out, now on his mind he had a feast.
For out of the Loach he darted, with the engine on but low;
    The chopper blades turning slowly now, just waiting but to go.

The young man like so many, most likely less than twenty years;
    Ran across the yard and true to form, certainly showed no fear.
That's when I saw what he was after, his target of the day;
    A scrawny thing they called a chicken, as it headed for the hay.

It ran and ran, yet faster, the young man closing on his tail behind;
 As we above could only laugh, thinking he must have lost his mind.
The chicken ran into a corner, his end not too far now;
 The young man then ran around, what appeared to be a cow.

A water buffalo it turned out, was just grazing all the while;
 As those of us flying o'erhead, all we could do was smile.
The young warrior approached the chicken, his enemy soon to pay;
 He had it cornered now, moved in, while keeping the water
 buffalo at bay.

I saw him reach for the chicken, wings moving as it attempted to fly;
 The young man lunged and grabbed its legs, holding the
 quarry up so high.
He'd had his fun chasing o'er the farm, his paltry little lunch;
 It demonstrated yet once again, how wild those warrant officers were:
 A courageous, fearless bunch!

In all my days of flying there, I saw nothing quite the like;
 Of a young man landing behind the enemy's lines, as if but
 on a hike.
From a hundred feet above I saw, he had his lunch, just like food fast;
 But I couldn't help but wonder, if it might not be his last.

As he made his way back to the Loach, the Cobra rolled in hot;
 'Cause just a few hundred meters away, he saw movement:
 fortunately not a lot.
And as I pulled off to the west, the Loach pulled up rather a bit abrupt;
 The Cobra fired into that green stage, as if only to disrupt.

The young man's chase for lunch that day, nicely ended with success;
 Having flown a few missions beside these men, I'd come to
 expect no less.
The Loach pulled up and flew by me, the young fellow with his prize;
 Strung from the canopy top, fluttering wildly, I could only
 laugh so at its size.

For the chicken was but a mouthful, looked like feathers more than meat;
But I could see the glee, and heard the radio, blaring of his feat.
While some may think this story foolish, there's a lesson to throw out;
When we seek men who are fearless, you need only look for
those scouts.

For those who piloted the Loaches, were to all, a breed apart;
Seeking bunker complexes, enemy caches, they were always
quick to dart.
Just like a little hummingbird, from tree to tree, they flew;
They hunted the enemy, did their job, with bravery and spirit, too.

Those men, so young, of yesteryear—they were an emboldened lot;
They knew no fright, would hover, appearing invincible to gunshot.
They were a different class of men, American's all, but more;
Incapable of being rattled, while hugging that jungle floor.

It's hard to look back now, and give it just perspective;
For many did their jobs too well, and for that, their lives did give;
So we can live a life of ease, enjoy liberty and freedom dear;
Paid for by these young men back then, who showed never any fear.

Nui Ba Den

Nui Ba Den is a singular mountain sitting close to the Vietnamese Cambodian border in what was then III Corps. It was on the route for most of our missions to and from our Area of Operations in Cambodia. Atop the mount sat a radio relay station, call sign Rustic Alpha, that was our lifeline. And much like the anomalies that permeated that war, we owned the top and the bottom of the mountain while the Viet Cong owned most of the middle of it, a labyrinth of tunnels and paths with boulders the size of small houses. It was always a welcome sight on returning from a mission.

Lonely sentinel in the sky;
Standing in the night.
A mountain there, by grace of God;
To help us in the fight.

Was great to see en route back home;
Passing by when letting down.
Descending through the pitch black air;
And down below lay Tay Ninh town.

Some lights, for few had been
Seen out across the fence
While riding off to work
O'er Cambodian jungle, ever dense.

Best to see on the way to land;
For when we passed the other way;
Was only then we gave a thought;
Wanting to see but once again.

Like a maiden, out there alone;
Standing quiet as statues might;
Rising 'bove those rice fields burning;
Was such a wondrous sight.

And when we saw it twice;
On a mission 'cross the fence;
Knew then we'd lived for more;
To fly another mission hence.

We owned the top back then;
The VC half way up that slope;
Our friends all 'round below;
A strange predicament of hope.

And today a park is there;
With music from the ski lift chairs;
An incongruous sight
For once, that beacon in that war.

And as you ride the slope serene;
Men died to own the crest;
So we could have a line;
Cast o'er Cambodia to do our best.

Back then was Rustic Alpha
Atop that guidepost in the night
So we could but report
Those troubles had in sight.

Loved to see it headed east
When mission was but done;
When heading to our bed
Flying down the throat of sun.

With brightness blinding up ahead
Was grand to look down as we passed
But knowing mostly, then and there
That trip would not then, be our last.

And as I passed that mount so tall
On fini flight, the last to fly;
Was a beauty to behold
Cragged precipice, piercing sky.

Body Count

Body count was the term used throughout Southeast Asia during the war with dubious results. This particular term was used primarily by ground forces while KBA, or *k*illed *by a*ir, was used in assessing results of airstrikes, gunship attacks and helicopter assaults. To some extent, the body count was used in supporting our thesis of pacification, or the determination of what areas in the war zone were securely in our hands and those of our allies.

I detested the use of this form of "accounting" then as I do now. The entire process was in dire need of auditing to say the least. In all too many cases, those commanders who counted the highest were subsequently, at a later time when requested, provided the greatest assets of air support, for example. Ho Chi Minh said that he was willing to lose 10 men for every one of ours and we should have heeded his wanton approach to war, or steeled ourselves to stay the course. In any event, this exercise proved to be one of futility and I doubt that its sinister message will be repeated in military or media circles in the future.

Of all that war's absurdities, one certainly led the rest;
    For body count was callous, and far from an idea best.
As this accounting exercise, that some thought would win the war;
    Unfortunately this was not the case, for the figures added poor.

Some hated this while others, attracted to such a macabre skill;
    Would double or triple, might even quadruple, the number
        of their kill.
Inflation may have had its start in this abhorrent quest;
    For those who could count the highest, thought that they
        were likely best.

The travesty of this endless game, held in esteem but by a few;
    Never won a battle or the war, cause the enemy most oft withdrew.
I'm only left to wonder, how many trails of blood,
    Or body parts were added, to make the numbers flood.

But in the mid of April, Nineteen Hundred and Seventy Five;
    Mattered little then the body count—just those who were alive.
And held onto the ground then, occupying across the land;
    When what really counted—not numbers dead—but enemy
        left to stand.

Made no difference in the end, just how high that sum had tallied;
    When the enemy forces in the North, to the South, they just
        had rallied.
But of all the issues surrounding, the infamous body count;
    Those numbers, no matter how high they were, could no
        more than just amount

To pieces of paper, meaningless, dropped to the bottom line;
    But for those of McNamara's ilk, wanted numbers—Oh! So fine.
And in the end if Fort Puzzle, the Puzzle Palace, chose;
    No doubt that some of those bodies, must surely have arose.

Because with numbers obviously bloated—far, far more than a few score—
    There'd be none alive in Southeast Asia today—Yes, that's
        right—
                    No People More!
So if this practice was worthless, and such a gruesome drill;
    I can only now but wonder, why we added up the kill.

For pieces of bodies were counted, when airstrikes were soon done;
    I can only assume those carcasses, were rotting in the sun;
While someone made his rounds, to count the grisly gore;
    But more than likely a paper pusher, then simply added more.

Of all the things I saw and did, even kept notes in my log;
    Those *K*illed *by* *A*ir or KBA, leave me still somewhat agog.
No wonder then that many protested, trying to preserve some
    humanity for all;
For those who thought up this ritual, must have been Neanderthals.

Hanoi Jane

Of all those ill-gotten lives, that I'd certainly rather not be:
Is that of the infamous Hanoi Jane—far better her than me.
I've known so many who label her, a vile and treasonous traitor;
And even I have never understood, why she went to view
our bombs' craters.

She looked through enemy gun sights, to target
our country's planes;
Pointed weapons of war skyward t'ward us—
was she then just insane?
She was aiming the antiaircraft gun, as if to shoot us down;
Guess the best that can be said, her mind was probably not then sound.

'Cause if that's not the actual case, then I still today wonder why;
She should not now be punished, perhaps even, just left to die.
Seems treason was and is no longer, seen as politically incorrect;
When folks who give favor to the enemy, their lives are not then wrecked.

Of course, some may say defamation, about her truthfully
soiled family name;
But I can't see how it's called slander, when she brought on
so much shame.
To all Americans who fought for freedom, and for those
who protested alike;
I've not seen a much lower life form, from that
long ago distant fight.

Meeting happily with our enemies, who held seat
in the North at Hanoi;
Currying favor with those who held our POWs, those
who tortured with such joy.
She met with the North Vietnamese, who sought to kill us
with much glee;
Think you'll understand this better now, as it could have
then been me.

Most probably today some would say, that we shouldn't assign
to her blame;
A young person like that long ago, who so sullied her
well-known name.
The stories today most surely abound, about different
things she did;
While some might be exaggerated, there are others
that made her bed.

I have quite a very strong feeling, that if many pilots of my kind;
Had one more flight with ammunition, forgiveness to her,
would not be on their minds.
'Tis indeed a strange world, when a person just like her;
Comes to know great wealth and health, but is to many, just a cur.

Thank goodness I believe strongly, that God has a plan for us;
While I, therefore, should not judge her now, I don't find that
much of a plus.
For those who were alive to view her, they may now choose
to show some kindness;
While so many of our brothers, don't forget, departed there
just lifeless.

And as we take leave of this subject, that's frankly
not worth much print;
I cannot understand why some applaud her—have not,
even now, a glint.
So today I may suggest a thought, for those who think
I'm mean;
Picture her today in a Taliban gun pit, and then
you may begin to glean.

That if someone from America, went today to Afghanistan;
Sat there at an antiaircraft gun, and aimed at an American man.
Perhaps the understanding then, would align somewhat more
with mine;
For those who never quite understood, might then view her
as but swine.

Regardless of where politicians rest, on questions and matters of war;
It will never be right for an American to give aid, or
to help the enemy score.
No need to take this further, because you've got the gist;
There should be penalties given to those, who give our enemies an assist.

Author's Note:

This poem was written in October, 2001, prior to our capturing
an American man in Afghanistan fighting on the side of the Taliban.
The facts, as I know them, are that he was there of his own free
will, armed and prepared to kill American fighting men. My
thoughts are pretty basic—enough said.

In My Face

Once while in Air Force uniform, many long years ago;
    I was walking through an airport—on my way home, to go;
When a peacenik jammed a flower, right in front of my face;
    Then I asked him, quite courteously, to give me some needed space.

He accused me of killing, women and babies by scores;
    Guess he thought he had me pegged, as one who'd back out
        the door;
So I asked him then to remove, the small flower in his hand;
    Not wanting to make a scene, but not liking his rude grandstand.

But he persisted, the flower there—my face was just in front;
    I said then rather brusquely—remove it now, or pull back a stump.
He most immediately removed, his bright posy very fast;
    And I imagine I'm the pilot, he tried that stunt on last.

War's End

Of those forces besieged, Cambodians helped in years past;
It was sad that our efforts, in that land did not last;
As our struggle for all, proved only good for a few;
As we departed our brethren, and bid our adieu.

T'was Nineteen Seventy—Three, the 15th of August;
That's when Congress declared, that long war a bust.
At noon on that day, the last flight there was flown;
And sadly our history, in that land was then sown.

The Vet: What Price Paid?

Shell shock, battle fatigue, PTSD[5];
No matter what the name.
Some seemed to overcome it;
While others suffered blame.

The senses became absorbed and numb;
Smell, taste, touch, hearing and sight;
To input—overloaded, succumbed;
For some in combat—was their plight.

Perhaps more a function of DNA;
Just what your genes contained.
How some, they managed to hold at bay;
While others became, quite unrestrained.

'Twas true the training may have helped;
Than being shipped out, right away.
But in the end, when gore was seen;
The smell of gunpowder and TNT[6]—
They made the senses pay.

---

[5]   Various labels have been attached: shell shock in World War I; battle fatigue
in World War II; and PTSD or *Post Traumatic Stress Disorder* in Vietnam
and Southeast Asia

[6]   TNT = trinitrotoluene

The whistle of incoming rounds, hitting close to home;
The sound and flash, of mortars and rockets in the night;
The smell of oil, of JP4[7] and avgas[8], at the airdrome;
The sight of napalm, gave some such fright.

The heat from radios galore;
A safety line in battle;
'Twas ever nice to hear the sound;
Of voices, not just prattle.

The salt stained flight suits and uniforms;
The smell of sweat, hours old;
Dirt imbedded in your clothes;
Your senses drained, if truth were told.

The blossom of artillery fire;
The crack of gunfire, ever so dire;
The sight of men lain, on the ground;
New feelings then, forever found.

The sound of a foreign language;
The nasal twangs of voice;
And through it all, you cherish only;
Your frame intact—rejoice!

Mail and tapes from home did help;
The news of old, familiar days;
To some, brought aid and comfort;
To others, their souls to flay.

---

[7]   JP4 = jet propellant, a kerosene based fuel used in jet engines
[8]   Avgas = aviation gasoline, usually 100 octane or lower grade gasoline used
      in propeller driven aircraft

The sight of choppers taking off;
Young men heading off to act;
The charging of machine guns
For the enemy—to gain contact.

Those helicopters going whop, whop;
Those blades churning in thick air;
Young men and women squandered so;
Looking back, was not so fair.

The flak vest that you sat on;
The survival vest you wore;
Protection for your body;
For what, fate had in store.

The long hours flush with adrenaline;
And others with alcohol;
No wonder after some combat missions;
Wanted to party more with all.

And then there was some loneliness;
One's inability to live with himself;
The strain and pangs of loved ones missed;
Feelings placed, for a time on a shelf.

And bombs delivered, right on target;
The plumes of dark gray smoke;
Perhaps some secondaries[9] yet;
To help the enemy croak.

---

[9]   Secondaries = secondary explosions; i.e., enemy ammunition, POL
(*p*etroleum, *o*il and *l*ubricants), etc., detonating as the result of the primary
explosion from a bomb, rocket, napalm or artillery round

And when it comes right down to it;
The taking of some lives;
While few rejoice, and some recoil;
Fight or flight—your choice of drives.

Some reveled in the glory;
If that is what it's called;
While most just did their jobs as best
When in the war—not so enthralled.

Hearing some call out in anguish;
Dealing with their untold pain.
Some could not be helped soon enough;
What price paid, by those who're sane?

No surprise, that some are found today;
Along life's trodden ways.
Some vets, unshaven, soiled and hungry;
Could not cope, in the returning fray.

For some, was just a flesh wound;
For others, quite the more;
Emotions and your senses;
So overwhelmed in war.

While some have been quite fortunate;
Putting locks on those gates in their minds;
As most have moved on in life, while changed;
Others have yet, themselves to find.

So if you have not been there;
Hold judgment from the talk;
Shrink from opinions offered;
Unless you've walked the walk.

And if you come upon a vet;
Down on his luck again;
He, or she, may have been a hero;
Once upon a time, back then.

Return to Cambodia

In March, 1999, I was fortunate to return to Southeast Asia. This was indeed the trip of a lifetime and much less intense than my previous Department of Defense sponsored tour.

A land of serenity, near to my heart;

A land of great beauty, was sad to depart

Was years long ago, in a war now long past;

'Twas so glad to be back, hope not for the last.

Remembrance

Written on the occasion of our third Rustic Reunion
in San Antonio, Texas, in 2002.

For those who've been in combat;
Who've seen the sights of war;
Who've climbed a hill, while shot at;
Or flown missions, by the score.

For those who've come back, fit and strong;
No scars from wounds, to be seen;
To those certainly who, received a Purple Heart;
Their blood given at, the battle scene.

For those who've watched, the rockets glare;
Hit the ground, to keep their lives;
And those on ships, and in supporting roles;
Who gave those in combat, drive.

We must remember brothers;
Men who sacrificed their prime.
And toast to those, in Heaven now;
'Cause they passed before their time.

Could in many cases, have been our life;
Called away before we'd thrived;
Who might have gone before our brothers;
But instead, we've lived our lives.

So it's here we are, to raise a toast;
To those: who've gone before.
Who've paved the way, when we depart;
To better prepare us, for what's in store.

And to those of us who're here;
To raise a glass, out of respect.
Look also 'round the room, at others near;
Who flew with you, when we sought to protect.

Fellow Rustics who flew o'er Cambodia;
Trying to make the world a better place;
To those who came, from that land we hold dear;
Tonight, to those here, who won that race.

We saw the ground then, down close at hand;
The Mekong but flowing, slowly by;
As we turned and pulled, fired rockets;
Piercing holes through Cambodia's sky.

To the pilots, interpreters and intell all;
Those in maintenance and munitions back then;
And to those who strived, to keep our airplanes flying;
So that we could join, tonight again.

And lest not forget the men today;
Who're standing here, along beside;
Just as in those years, so long ago;
Our true brothers, still locked in stride.

For as you look around tonight;
And see friends, from days gone by;
Give thought that probably, one of them;
May be the reason, you did not die.

For all of us worked some target;
That had it not been blown;
May have been the man, went unscathed below;
Whose bullet, our fate then, might have sown.

So to those who've gone before;
And to men who're with us now tonight;
And to those, who could not make it here;
We all tempted fate, and fought the fight.

We raise a glass to all our brothers;
Whether past, present or afar;
To the Rustics and the many others;
Who know what it was, to have been in war.

And when I'm no longer amongst you;
When you raise your glass of cheer.
You need only look up skyward;
For my spirit will surely be there.

'Cause my days of flying as a Rustic FAC;
Were among those I cherished the most.
So enjoy your night and our longtime friends;
As you rise to make this toast.

Peace

Peace for all—a most desirable state of mind:
    When those 'round the world cease fighting 'mongst mankind;
Living our lives—we can travel without fear;
    Cease to worry 'bout those that we hold so dear.

Would be a wonderful world in which to live:
    Where all would cease taking and only but give
Of themselves and their love shown to those here on earth;
    So that more who're around us could enjoy more mirth.

For children who go hungry more days than not;
    Who seldom have cold meals—let alone some hot;
And that we could eradicate more disease;
    Lay no more mines that result in amputees.

To live in a world where all have more freedom;
    No attacks of terror that leave us so numb;
For all to pray to Jesus, Allah or God;
    Such is my prayer, as through this life I plod.

Having fought long ago in a far away land
    With men who became like my brothers—yes, a band.
I know that I speak for all who served there with me;
    Pray that someday we live in peace for us to see.

So that children of all come to love one another;
    Regardless of color, language, culture—like brothers;
Cease this endless round of brutalization to others;
    So that all may work together—fathers and mothers.

Would be a beautiful, breathtaking, sight to behold;
    For all the leaders in our world to take steps so bold;
To live in peace going forth—'tis a dream that I hold;
    To cease wars that are hot—as well as those that are cold.

Most would say it's impossible to have such a world;
    I believe it's a hope to convey to boys and girls;
For if taught to the young as opposed to such hatred;
    Peace then would abound, and of such wars we'd be rid.

While this is a picture I would most love to see;
    I'd settle for this as a beginning—with much glee;
Would be a grand state to live in—altogether in peace;
    To have no knowledge of war—or of weapons' expertise;

So our children could be raised, grow up and live not in fear.
    They could travel the world—not stay only where they are near;
To use airplanes once again with no dread of hijacking;
    Enjoy cultures of others and freedoms: with little lacking.

It would be a wonderful world if this came to be true;
    I'd settle for better than that which we have—long overdue;
While I doubt that I'm alive to see the best for such peace;
    I'd welcome an improvement today—of war, a decrease.

It would be a lofty goal for our children to enjoy:
    Such a state of real peace and love, with no weapons deployed.

ON SEPTEMBER 11TH

As We Move Forward

Dedicated to those who lost their lives on September 11, 2001,
and in the days following from the terrorist attacks in New York
City, at the Pentagon and in the airplane crash in Pennsylvania,
and to those who have had their lives changed forever as
a result of these despicable acts.

When we awoke on Tuesday morning, another day in America so bright;
    Little did we know that we were in for such momentous and
    dreadful sights:
Explosions and catastrophe, loss of life on that splendid morn;
    From those who hold our land, indeed our way of life, in such
    vast scorn!

The attacks in New York City, that killed many and brought such ruin;
    That snatched so many lives, for all too many families and yet
    all too soon.
It's hard to describe the pain and anger, throughout our nation
    that is now felt;
    But amongst our hopes today are that fierce blows will soon
    be dealt.

For as long hours now stretch to days, for those valiant attempts at rescue;
    Our great hope first for the many, now but dwindles to the few.
And for those who at the Pentagon, those who work to keep us secure;
    Along with all too many that day, lives forever changed while
    families endure:

The pain and anguish for those who wait to see if loved ones are alive;
    While many others died in such circumstances—'tis not kind
        to describe.
And as we hear of others arrested and some that are now sought;
    We can only hope that punishment is meted out for what's
        been wrought.

But the grief to many families, of sons and daughters lost;
    Of fathers, mothers, brothers, sisters, husbands and wives—
        all an untold cost.
The damage to our economy and to our freedom dear;
    Make no mistake about it—Our enemies will soon know fear.

Let to those who now have raised, their wrath against us all;
    Know a sleeping giant has been awakened—America will stand tall!
There is nothing quite so sacred, as to our homeland have attacked;
    And to those radicals both here and abroad—one message:
        We'll fight back;

Stronger than's ever been seen before—for they lit a flame quite dire;
    One that will burn them and turn their cause into a lost quagmire.
Because there's no greater force: Than to live free as we do;
    As those terrorists on the one plane, they most likely dealt with
        a few

Men and women, who were brave, not at all unlike you and me;
    Who were willing to sacrifice, as many others have past, for us
        to continue free!
And to those who wish to take from us, our loved ones—Oh, So Dear!
    I'm certain they'll get the message: That we do not quake with fear.

To those who hit on the eleventh of September, using terror as
    their tool;
    They'll soon come to learn what we have for them, is far more
        than just ridicule.

I have no doubt we'll stand united, and charge into this fight;
> As has never been done before in our history, that is long and
> will grow again bright.

And while we're gathering forces and developing our battle plan;
> Let's learn from our experiences past that have cost too many a man.
And if our civil liberties are trimmed a bit, in the long run, for the best;
> Keep in mind 'tis better than to lose them all, or fail in our just quest.

Let's keep our anger aimed correctly, at only those who seek us to kill;
> And not attack others, who've but come to America, with
> their hopes and skills;
Just as our forebears did before us, many years ago long past;
> But let's target only those we want—not jump the gun too fast.

It's all too easy to paint such terrorists with a stroke all too broad brush;
> But recall that some of their heritage, also came here to avoid
> being crushed.
In that regard we must remember to move forward with much care;
> Gain intelligence, form a plan, assemble, attack—but do not spare;

The lives of terrorists who've taken from us, but for so short awhile;
> Our serenity, our way of life—but we'll overcome those vile.
And as a veteran, like many others, I humbly do but ask:
> That mistakes we've made in times before are not repeated
> from our past;

That we tackle this war with commitment—so that America will always last!
> My hopes are for our country—that we have heard in our
> land, final blasts.
And to those who obviously fantasize that their terror will have
> such gain;
> Let's send to them a message clear: Those who died did not
> do so in vain!

September 14, 2001

Heroes Best Defined

In times gone by we've used the word
Hero—applied quite freely;

Assigned to movie stars—absurd;
To sports figures—now, really!

These folks but for us entertain;
Many chasing but the green;

And for them I have no disdain;
They like mostly to be seen.

But among us, has now been shown;
There are men and women great;

They rush to victims when they moan;
Fighting fire before too late.

They're police, firefighters, caring
For all others in their midst.

They're men and women—so daring;
And when recently, they didst

But give their lives, so many called
In New York City, stars defined

Firemen, policemen—one and all!
Our heroes indeed did shine!

Vietnam Revisited—
Lessons Learned

This is dedicated to all those who lost their lives in the war in Southeast Asia and to those whose lives, both there and on the home front, were forever altered. Hopefully many of the lessons learned from that guerilla war will be transferred to the War on Terrorism that today confronts America.

It amazes me in interviews—'tis said nothing like this before;
> Has ever been experienced by our country—stated by commentators galore.
But there are indeed similarities, and many of those in reality abound;
> 'Cause when in Vietnam, terror was ever present as rockets rained around.

'Twas disconcerting then, when the only thing we discovered
> Was a mortar tube buried to its mouth, and a timer on it recovered.
The enemy was faceless then, much the same as it is now;
> One of the many problems then, so that people would but cow.

'Cause it mattered little, whether NVA, Khmer Rouge or Viet Cong;
> But was difficult to distinguish friend from foe, in order to get along.
And indeed today the enemy: are terrorists who can easily come and go.
> With our meaningless immigration laws and those only enforced just so.

Now when the numbers of aliens illegal only seem to mount;
>   We take a census, change the laws, now legal, their votes do count.
We now need to identify more than ever before those who are our
worst foes;
>   Much as with those in Vietnam, where many fought and gave
>   so many years ago.

There were in that conflict in a far off land, problems: most times
ones new;
>   And living here now as we do today, hope we comprehend
>   from those past clues.
One of the worst: intelligence then was much akin to a sieve;
>   And for the lack of it, abuse of it, many were the lives we did give.

The enemy knew our plans then, as many who were there can
readily attest;
>   We may as well have had them on our distribution list as they
>   came by info best.
The human intelligence, or "humint," was certainly there most
lacking;
>   And when our troops did engage, we oft times craved adequate
>   backing.

One of the greatest ironies was of America's funding and fiscal planning;
>   When at the end of the year, airstrikes were plentiful; easy
>   was the manning.
However, the next day, beginning of the new fiscal year, we could
not get supported;
>   Even for firefights when lives were at risk, missions were
>   commanded aborted.

The idea we were told was to save our strength so we would not run out;
>   Of money to fund the fighters and bombs—so at times we
>   lacked the clout.
If we're going to fight a war, then let Congress meet and declare it;
>   As opposed to dancing 'round semantics, and calling it a conflict.

We were good at getting into it then, but had few objectives clear;
    And gathered our forces together, so that they would in most
        cases be near.
We were most vulnerable as we are today, in many respects alike;
    Our lines of communication, our bases, our people—easy
        enough to strike.

We faced a committed enemy, the likes of which before in Korea only seen;
    One who was ever ready to die, as in his next life to be all the
        more keen.
And worst of all we served one year tours, as if it would end it all;
    When you fight a war, send the best, and stay till all the
        enemy fall.

Not to get combat experience for the many, for only after they are all back;
    Unable to retain and pay all those soldiers and pilots then, a
        realistic fact.
We fought our war in comfort, for most with the base exchange nearby;
    Movie theaters, a swimming pool and clubs for the troops to
        get high.

My father who fought in World War Two, spending three years in
    a foreign land;
    Never could fathom how we fought that war, not surprised
        that we got canned.
But there should be limits for the troops, for such comforts in a war zone;
    At least one reason comes to mind: for some most likely had it
        better than home.

As for surgical airstrikes we had our share, for some of the fighters
    were grand;
    In virtually all instances, what we needed most: ground troops
        to take a stand.
Not to have men fight for the same hill, not once, but to tackle it more;
    To lose lives first, and then when up it again, just to lose a few
        more score.

Such airstrikes are great if infrastructure is there, to go after again
and again;
But when the foe moves swiftly with only small targets, is
certainly hard to win.
Such attacks worked in Iraq, with buildings and radar sites in abundance;
But that's not the case in Afghanistan, with no massing of
troops for ordnance.

If a thousand guerillas or terrorists, go in as many directions;
Are we then going to drop one thousand bombs, all with
numerous corrections?
Such was the case in Southeast Asia when such groupings of troops
were few;
An occasional truck, or sampan, and thus, our enemy there knew

That technologically advanced forces could be attacked where they
but massed;
And satellites were of little use, with the enemy using tactics
from our past.
Because we fought in Southeast Asia much as the Redcoats once did;
In our own Revolutionary War, when as Colonials we made
our bid

To seek freedom in which we believed so much, we were ready to
hit and run;
But this war today is one of wits, commitment, and not limited
to guns.
Much as guerillas today are taught, as well as Special Forces and
our Seals;
So is not a new concept to deal with, but we must approach
with zeal.

And if the executive order, as to assassinations needs to be shelved;
Then do it now, attack the snake at its head, into the terrorists'
niche to delve.

If we think our mighty forces, give pause, to the terrorists do impress;
  They most probably think as a target rich environment, to
  hit and put in distress.

We need as a nation to grasp a few things: how these terrorists
  most likely think;
  Before trying to attack with these weapons of ours, they may
  but present a chink;
In our overall security, now that forces are to be spread around the world.
  As we're marching off to this battle, with pride and America's
  flags unfurled.

I'm all for coalition building, as was even done somewhat in Vietnam;
  Not enough for sure, we had others fight, such as the Aussies
  and the Koreans.
But we need to understand why these radicals fight, so as to stamp
  this out;
  To gain some insight to the rationale of these attacks—so we
  may then fully rout;

To separate these Islamic Fundamentalists from the true tenets of
  their religion;
  For they have taken the convictions of many, and made into
  an abomination.
At the heart of Islam is a true belief of peace, for to kill one is like
  all humanity;
  But these fundamentalists are committed, and not to a cause
  of insanity.

They abhor our use of their Holy Lands, where our troops based a
  decade ago;
  They detest rights for women, pornography and our way of
  life just so.
These are among some of the causes for them to join and rally around;
  And as with many a war, is easy to gather, for poor people do
  abound.

For with those who live in poverty, they have little but to lose;
    And when they maintain so dearly their beliefs—lives are but
        free to use.
We need to be careful that our forces strong, are directed not against Islam;
    For the true believers in that religion, are far removed from
        enemies in Vietnam.

But those who are in the mountains of Afghanistan, and other
    countries far and wide;
    'Tis not so difficult to strike again, and then go to ground and hide.
This is most likely but another round in a war, that is to be long fought;
    Need look back to the bombing in ninety-three, when war was
        then first brought

To the World Trade Center, was their first attack, when we should
    have begun
    To ferret out their networks, seeking then more money to
        have them on the run.
But not much to be gained by criticizing that now, or the attack
    on the USS Cole;
    It's time to form our alliances, attack this movement and create
        our role.

Of those things that were most lacking, in Vietnam way back then;
    Intelligence and security and the unfettered will to win.
Rules of engagement remain a nerve ending, ever still so raw;
    'Cause was difficult there to take fire and not return it—
        as those in power saw.

They put our troops in harm's way, as I hope is not done now;
    While restricting them from fighting, many times did not allow;
To pursue across some imaginary line on a map, to keep happy
    world opinion;
    We let those who attacked just hit and run—like the leaders
        of 911's hellions.

So we have today for our children, the battle of our lives;
    Make no mistake about it—those terrorists don't lack drive!
They're committed to destroying, changing forever our way of life;
    To overcome passengers on a plane, to slit women's throats
        with a knife.

So we're kidding ourselves if we think these terrorists, we should apprehend;
    More appropriately a most strong message we need to certainly send.
This is not a venue for the capture, and of spectacular trials;
    I would submit that our best course is to them: death and denial.

And for those who don't know the difference, between two similar words;
    One should be our choice of action, the other is quite absurd:
For the chicken is "dedicated" to the eggs it does produce;
    But the pig is absolutely "committed" to the bacon it gives
        for our use!

I would submit that in Vietnam, dedication was the effort made;
    For we lacked resolve, were weak in the end, oft times but few
        were saved.
These are among but a few of those things, will stick in my mind
    till death;
    For when we fought in Southeast Asia, many people were left bereft.

Of those tools of war like hot pursuit and reasonable ROE[10];
    For we tried there to fight a clean conflict, for all the world to see.
We didn't learn much from the French, who at Dien Bien Phu surrendered;
    And the Russians learned little from either of us, as in Afghanistan
        they bolted.

---

[10]   ROE = Rules of Engagement

So there are many lessons I hope we've grasped, not only for troops
    in the field;
    But we as a nation must realize, unite and come prepared to wield
The sword of justice against these terrorists, come committed to win;
    And not as in Southeast Asia, letting many in power with
        words but spin

The news of the day, and progress, as some viewed it from their chairs;
    For these recent attacks have conveyed gravity and brought
        the situation near.
And when all is said and done, with the resemblances of the past;
    There's a good reason that few have raised issues from Southeast
        Asia, aghast.

It troubles me now, as it always will, that we didn't fight there to win;
    And I only hope the fact that we lost there is not repeated again.
Now perhaps therein lies the reason, why most don't choose to look back;
    To the war in Vietnam for similarities, 'cause in that war we
        were sacked.

That, in itself, is most likely, a reason the terrorists have now come
    to hold;
    That when the going got rough, too many lives lost, America
        seemed to fold.
We're viewed by many across the world, as a soft and arrogant lot;
    'Cause amongst our losses in Southeast Asia, Cambodia and
        Laos, a blot

On our prior history of fighting, to the end as in World War Two;
    Many now look on us as a society only willing to lose a few.
We carried this fact into Desert Storm, seeking an admirable course in war;
    And used technology and tactics to kill the enemy more.

But was easier in the desert, with trucks lined up for miles;
> And the Republican Guards deep in their bunkers, could bomb
> > into a pile.
But we should not confuse this war in Iraq, for the one we are in now;
> As the will of these terrorists is to die for their cause, not
> > readily to bow.

These are not rabble in the desert, conscripts as many Iraqis were in Kuwait;
> These are committed guerillas, and we don't want to learn too late.
If we think we're fighting a civilized war, then civil libertarians will
> likely learn;
> > That prior conventional rules of war, these enemies of ours will spurn.

Biological, chemical, nuclear—whatever may wreak devastation.
> They are not opposed to using weapons, ones of mass destruction;
And with that to name a few targets—to get all of us better aware;
> Our sources of water, reservoirs, electric substations—not just to scare.

Our bridges, rail lines, dams, our food sources to us dear;
> Many are our vulnerabilities, and most of those are quite near.
And while we focus on commercial aviation, making pilots' doors so tight;
> Let's not forget chartered planes that as weapons are quite ripe.

For would only be not difficult for a group to charter such a jet;
> No flight attendants or passengers to overcome, to jump the
> > crew a good bet.
And some of these planes carry tons of fuel, not as much as those
> used at first;
> > But the catastrophe derived from their use could be but just as worse.

What we need as much as anything in America today: is an awareness
> not before seen;
> > To avoid complacency and the sense of security, as it has always been.
To go about our lives, but paying attention to those around us today;
> In order to foil such terrorists, working hard to keep them at bay.

But I hope that those in command today have the skill to glean
    from the past;
      That we'll attack in unrelenting fashion, not think winning
        with words just cast.
Because in Vietnam, as is today, we were indeed technologically sound;
      We even had sensors on the Ho Chi Minh Trail, to sniff urine
        when 'twas found.

And we introduced the smart bomb there, out in Cambodia with
    laser lights;
      But for many reasons in our history now past, we lacked the
        will to fight.
So I send these words of caution, to our people and those making decisions:
      Gather strength to endure, in this our fight, not simply thoughts
        of derision.

In closing these reflections, one concept most important, is simply
    that of time;
      For we live in a land of instant gratification, everyone turns on a dime.
These terrorists do not have a schedule, to which most Americans align;
      They are much like Ho Chi Minh in this regard—not to our
        generation confined.

This battle for ideals, most holy to them, as but with our fight long ago;
      Ho Chi Minh cared little whether he saw the victory, as he
        knew it would be so.
Therein lies this doctrine of commitment, to us such a foreign concept
    of time;
      And, therefore, we need to approach this—for us, quite a new paradigm.

But perhaps the greatest reason, not to link these attacks to Vietnam now;
      Is the fact that for many reasons, we lacked commitment then
        and how!

September 20, 2001

Author's Note:

As I sit here today on December 17, 2001, our forces, together with the alliances forged in Afghanistan and elsewhere, have succeeded in routing the Taliban for all practical purposes. The implementation of modern technology and execution of this war has been all but flawless.

That said, I am of the opinion that this will indeed be a long war. We as a nation, unfortunately, have acquired many enemies. I genuinely hope that our population steels itself for endurance and does not sit back and glory in the current instant gratification that we have achieved. It should also not go without saying that we should support our troops throughout this effort, no matter what the time element involved.

Who Should Fight?

It never ceases to amaze me;
When talk comes 'round to war;
That all too many can't wait to see;
Others heading to foreign shores.

So many folks say: not my son
Or daughter will join the fight.
Wouldn't want their young as only pawns;
Regardless of whether wrong or right.

As often happens, the war is bad;
For some—What a surprise!
Many would rather other parents be sad;
Than take the risks of cries.

While some just want to talk the talk;
Their boldness shrinks with fear;
As others are left to walk the walk;
When war encroaches near.

And history even revises truth:
For John Wayne did not serve;
In World War Two—That is the truth!
But as a reel* man he had nerve.

And, then there's Lyndon Johnson, too;
Who received the Silver Star:
For taking a flight o'er the Pacific blue;
Questions arise—did he ever see that war?

So while in America we enjoy today;
Our precious freedom—here;
Give thought to those who paved the way;
And gave up their lives so dear.

So when it comes right down to it;
When push now comes to shove;
Are you willing to show some real grit?
Or just sit back and be a dove?

'Cause many before made the sacrifice;
So we could live and love;
Have and had friends who paid a price;
Some now look down from above.

So give some thought to those before;
Who've given of themselves for us.
Should make the decision—easier the more;
To join or support our troops—a must!

* *"Reel" is correctly spelled.*

Osama

Osama's the culprit, of that to be sure;

And of one thing we know: he will not endure.

Spreading such terror—he's certainly no knave;

And as a result, he's holed up in a cave.

To others who may also like a surprise;

Suggest they sit back—watch bin Laden's demise.

So for those who elect to live by the sword:

Their poster—dead or alive, with a reward.

ALASKA

For almost two weeks in July, 2001, I had the pleasure of joining with two other pilots and flying across much of Alaska and the western provinces of Canada—Yukon Territory, British Columbia and Alberta.

Joseph D. "Dan" Brown, III, M.D., in whose Cessna 210 we flew, was the flight surgeon—and a great one at that!—for a part of the time in which I served with the 149th Tactical Fighter Squadron flying F-105's. He is a man who loves adventure. Years ago I had, thanks to fellow Thud driver Bob Glover, joined with him and others associated with our fighter squadron on a week of white water rafting on the Colorado River through the Grand Canyon.

Holcombe A. J. "Hoc" Hughes, is a fighter pilot's fighter pilot, a fellow aviator with whom I would fly in any plane, anytime, and to anywhere of his choosing. A veteran of F-84's and F-86's, he is one of those rare pilots who possesses a sixth sense in the air, resulting in consistently excellent judgment. As with most pilots, that good sense is, in great part, a tribute to his thorough planning while on the ground.

It is with these two men that I joined in Anchorage, Alaska, after my good friend, Bob Glover, who had flown with them to that point, had to depart and return to Virginia. As we made our way across the grandeur that is Alaska the trip became an adventure. I departed in Calgary, Canada, and flew home commercially. There are indeed old, bold pilots—and these are them!

Anchorage

As you come upon Anchorage, set in a bowl;
You soon are convinced of God's most admirable role;
For the mountains are lush, unbelievably green;
The high waterfalls plenty, are fed by the streams.

Just outside this city are glaciers of beauty;
Pools of blue and green water, small but so many;
But the puzzle of it all, is those who surmise;
That there is no God, because they can't see His eyes.

Then you look around here, and His bounty you find;
All around Alaska, that He made for mankind.
The small seaplanes abound, at Spenard and Lake Hood;
The convenience behold—'tis not far from the woods;

To go hiking, camping, fishing, sightseeing, too;
Enjoy the big country sky, that sometimes is blue;
But for those souls who come here, they surely must see;
The greatness and grandeur, that surround you and me.

You may come to Alaska, forlorn, with but hope;
But you must either leave soon, or head for the slopes;
For there's flat-land galore, but the mountains take hold;
Don't come to Alaska, and expect to be told

To just stay in the cities, and shop in the stores.
You must see the back-country, to the iced Arctic shores.

On to Fairbanks

Fly by Mount McKinley, a white mountain so grand;
'Tis best to see it's face close—come to understand;
That God in His grace, made these sights for us all;
They surround in Alaska, He sought to enthrall.

When the mountain is "out," it is great to behold;
Such an immense work of Nature, none are too old
To enjoy its vast beauty, is to know and believe
That He's always with us, though we can't clearly see.

To know that He's here—is decidedly enough;
But for most 'tis a problem, 'cause not seeing is tough.
Then come to Alaska, and you'll come to believe;
That He's most certainly here, for all to perceive.

For today we've departed the Turnagain Arm;
Have struck out for Fairbanks, the plane's out of the barn.
Cook Inlet at six o'clock, not far behind me;
We're headed to Fairbanks, and then Arctic Sea.

These are, undeniably, not those days of old;
When pioneers and trappers set forth in the cold.
For today I'm with two good friends, pilots are we;
How wonderful and lucky, it is to be me.

Two men who're in the front seat, old pilots are they;
Who are more careful now, than perhaps yesterday.
But with care we are heading, far up in this land;
For no better reason, than 'tis the northernmost stand.

So much better to fly, than as Eskimos would;
To the north of Alaska, 'cause we only could.
See more of God's majesty, He made for us all;
Behold the rivers and woods, snow covered mounts tall.

Since passing three thousand feet, we've been in the clouds;
'Tis much like life's voyage, when we're troubled and bowed.
When sometimes we're confused, merely like in a fog;
We sometimes discover, that we're sunk in a bog;

Same as with the clouds, that we are flying in now;
Just like the murk of milk, when it comes from the cow.
But as pilots on instruments and compass we find;
That our flight is secure and provides peace of mind.

But why can't on this earth, why can't some folks see?
That God's but an instrument, a compass for me.
When passing Denali, we broke in the clear;
A tap on my leg, from my friends that are dear.

The dazzling sun's rays, on the clouds' layers all 'round;
And small lakes below us, once again now abound.
No roads and cars, thank goodness, to see down below;
'Tis only God's beauty, and 'tis fine to be so.

We're here at ten thousand, with blue sky above;
'Tis difficult to sit here, and not come to love;
My fellow man, and His vast wonders cast 'round:
All in Alaska, what God's made so abounds.

Just like in life, in the clouds there is hope;
For when we break out, 'tis a wonderful stroke;
Not only just luck, as some would believe;
But 'tis God's holy plan—for both you and me.

The land is so beautiful, now green down below;
The brown muddy streams, rambling thus to and fro;
The puffs of ivory clouds, that float here and there;
Just like the small problems, that I left way back where.

But as pilots we fly 'round them, below and above;
Just like those life's problems, that o'ercome with love.
It's sad that more people aren't pilots as we;
'Cause from my perspective, 'tis so easy to see.

If only we could learn, to fly straight and true;
To trust always in God, we'd soon see the blue;
In life a compass for heading, 'tis all we need;
An instrument we can, easily, find in Thee.

We're now losing altitude, closing with ground;
We're landing at Fairbanks—a new town we've found.
The mountains on the left, as we come in to land;
Simply more of God's beauty—so delightful and grand.

The airport's ahead, and the runway's in sight;
The days are so long here, but we'll soon spend the night.
So up to Alaska, you surely must come;
To see this spacious land of the Midnight Sun.

The sky now ahead, is so turquoise blue now;
You just have to wonder, the why and the how;
When His touch forged the mountains, and all came to be;
What seems to be land of immense infinity.

The small town's right ahead, the clouds now but few;
I'll plan for tonight—look for tomorrow anew.
The plane just set down, a sweet landing so clean;
The air is so fresh, 'tis a magnificent scene.

The sun's in the sky, brightly showing its beams.
Can understand what led folks, up here with their dreams.
For here in Alaska, where life is such fun;
Up soon to Alaska, you surely must come.

For most people that fly, that fly: Oh, so high;
Would surely agree that God's hands made the sky.
If all could just reach out, and only but touch;
Then so many folks would not doubt quite so much.

Fairbanks

To see the Nenana, a steamboat of old;
'Tis but to appreciate the miners of gold
Who came to Alaska, unbelievably bold;
Of their exploits, the poet, Robert Service told.

They came by the thousands, stuff of yellow to mine;
Some few came to be rich, while some lost their minds.
But to us, we enjoy much the history of old;
To come now to Alaska, you don't have to be bold.

'Tis good to see Fairbanks, on the banks of the Chena;
To eat salmon and halibut in a town that's much cleaner;
Than many such places in the Lower Forty-Eight;
'Tis time to come soon, 'tis not now too late.

Up to Alaska, in the north so far;
So to eat plenty and stand at a bar;
Here in the land of the Midnight Sun;
Up to Alaska, for fresh air and fun.

We went to the Pump House, an eatery so fair;
We sat at the bar, with not but a care;
My friends with cigars, while we savored the light;
Just 'fore midnight, the sun had then set out of sight.

Down the road after twelve, we chased, tried to locate;
Just o'er the horizon, orb now setting so late;
But the sun had outrun us, we couldn't catch then;
Turned around to head back, as in a few hours when;

That yellow ball would creep up, quite low in the sky;
Need a few hours sleep, before climbing on high.
Drive back to our rooms, with the shutters down tight;
To try to sleep in the dimmed light of the Alaskan "night."

The Next Great Flight

As we departed the lodge, where we'd spent that short night;
  Ran into some folks, who'd flown up for funeral rites;
Seems a good friend had passed, fellow—name of John McPhee;
  An old timer who'd fought, with the government you see.

He'd wanted to preserve the land, and the old way of life;
  Apparently died on the river, and not by a knife;
On his way downstream, to some court to sort out his fate;
  As he'd written "*Coming Into the Country*"—but maybe too late.

Out to the airport, for another pre-flight;
  Weather's just fine, and it's good to be right
    Here in Alaska, with people so fine;
  Cigars being smoked, drinking Jack Daniels and wine.

Hearing stories of old, from most our new friends;
  How men came to pan gold, and then died in the end;
    'Tis a great state to see, a country so grand;
  'Tis ours to behold, here God took His Stand.

Now ready for takeoff, down the runway we go;
  Propeller turning over, oh, but so slow!
    Off to McKinley, soon hoping to see
  God's awesome mountain, we hope it will be

"Out" today, snow-bright, to be viewed with much glee;
  The Mount's in the windscreen, clear as can be;
Ceiling's four thousand broken, with blue sky above;
  Up here in Alaska—we've come much to love.

Passing three thousand, just above, puffs of milk;
We're finding a nice hole, passing through just like silk.
Clear sky above, aviators dream of the blue;
With the spirit of pilots, simply put: Can Do.

The foothills below, are so beautiful, green;
All should come to Alaska, so that they may glean;
God's beauty and marvels, the truth to be told;
And inspiring grand stories, of the hard days of old.

Up in Alaska, the skies full of hope;
Just as in life, here up on the North Slope;
Finding holes in the clouds, just to get to the blue;
Learning from troubles, as in life, our passing on through.

For as pilots, we set heading, and plunge straight ahead;
Only storms and weather, do we but come to dread;
'Cause gas is our lifeblood, we're surely to watch;
Viewing God's land below, and His skies are top-notch.

One eighty's our heading, Mount McKinley to see;
Just as in life, sometimes backtracking as we;
Tend to go back and fetch, those sights that are good;
As only we wish, that sometimes we could.

The snow capped mountains are in front of us now;
For only our God, has the answers to how;
As we climb past ten thousand, sky clearing—bravo!
What a stunning sight, 'tis absurd to be low.

In this incredible land of the Midnight Sun;
'Tis grand to be here, having—Oh! So much fun;
With men who have served our country of old;
Fighter pilots who love God, if the whole truth were told.

It's clear to the west, broken clouds to the east;
God's now, as always around us, to say just the least.
We've turned to the north, the Mount's on our side;
To behold such splendor, as if on a glide.

Just like life's memories, in our six o'clock now;
As we sit here just wondering: it came to be how?
Up in Alaska, the sky, Oh! So fine;
Not gold now, but God's features, we come now to mine.

Up in Alaska, our path clear ahead;
Three hours to Barrow, thanks now: not by sled;
Our memories behind us, as in life, we go past;
Seems the good ones go more—only now, but so fast.

We have maps in the plane, to help if skies clear;
By our compass, our instruments, with God's hand—no fear;
We steer but ahead, as did those long ago;
But in air here on high, not on the ground as when slow.

Up here in Alaska, to travel by air;
Today with such height, staying clear of the bear.
The puffs of white cotton, we view from on high;
Such tufts of pure silk, as we pass them right by.

'Tis now miles per hour, the speed we come to abide;
Not by mach, we three of old, used when on fighter rides.
But more slowly we come, to take bits of our time;
To appreciate God's treasures, and life in our prime.

'Tis great to have friends, like the two just up front;
And the one lost in Texas, last week—but the brunt
It's today just hitting me, as I reflect and sit here;
'Tis those things in life—friends—to hold close and dear.

As pilots secure in our actions, since young;
Not much baggage we have now, when old to be brung;
For our paths and roads traveled, have been mostly straight;
We've gone 'round but few obstacles and steady of gait.

As pilots, 'tween two points, the straightest of lines;
We aim our nose now directly, as we have many times;
To arrive at our landing, safe and unscathed;
Just as in life's great journey, such is that which we crave.

The tundra we're o'er now, the foothills are few;
The land is such a clear green, it looks just like new;
The roads nonexistent, no lines to be seen;
Arctic Circle so close now, sights uncluttered to be gleaned.

Up here in Alaska, tundra now down below;
Thank goodness we're traveling, high and now slow;
For God's miracles below us most surely abound;
'Tis grand to be alive, and to look all around.

We're crossing the Yukon, a river so mild;
It looks from on high that it can't be that wild;
But from stories of old, when this river was ice;
As a passage when breaking up, 'twas not so nice.

The trees are now thinning, the ground turning brown;
The terrain getting rougher, below us—surrounds;
To the Brooks Range we head, but a short time away;
Thank goodness by airplane, and not now by sleigh.

The pilot's window flew open, awake now: I'm sure;
To slow down the airplane, is swiftly the cure;
Just like in life, I now feel so alive;
After small troubles pass, we get soon back in stride.

Catching a glimpse, of the pipeline below;
Today we land in Barrow, tomorrow at Prudhoe.
The peaks coming sharper, the land but more stark;
Best here in light of summer, not in winter of dark.

'Tis great to be a pilot, to have flown for so long;
As it's great to be right, more oft times than when wrong.
The doors of flying, have opportunities brought;
To those men and women, who have but so sought.

To have slipped bonds of earth for the beauty of blue;
To have witnessed God's majesty and sights, Oh! So new;
To find peace and such joy, experiences so nice;
In clear sky, white clouds, and a few times some ice.

One of the best decisions, many years made ago;
Was to join the U.S. Air Force, and not fly so slow;
Those times today long gone, many memories so fine;
I'd recommend to any, as would pilot friends of mine.

The Arctic Circle, that we just crossed down below;
Just a line on the map, not beneath in the snow;
The clouds now in abundance, are broken to o'ercast;
As a bed of smooth cotton, from on high we go past.

The Brooks Range underneath us, the map clearly shows;
But white mostly we see now, cold ice and the snow;
You have to wonder what was it, that led men up here;
Think I'll sit and ponder that thought, over my next beer.

Just as in life, occasionally richness is hidden;
Continuing on as in life, so troubles are smitten;
We need only go further, on trust to be sure;
Once again t'ward the clear, for clarity so pure.

The Brooks Range today, in the clouds down below;
Just as in life, when some dangers don't show;
We sit here and, in truth, can only but ask
Why God gave us life, and some improbable tasks.

Up here in Alaska, the horizon so clear;
Blue sky above now, clouds below and so near;
Up in the land of such imposing sights;
'Tis but summer now, so no Northern Lights.

As if on a glacier, the clouds slightly rising;
Examining the beauty, in hopes of no surprising;
Eleven thousand feet now, we climb a bit more;
Through those o'ercast clouds, we have yet to bore.

We're closing on Barrow, as those who've come here before;
Wiley Post, Will Rogers, but not too many more;
'Tis a land of few people, 'bove the Circle up here;
With walrus, whale, polar bear, and best yet: more than eight reindeer.

Up here in Alaska, where things seem so small;
Up here in Alaska, where God seems so tall;
Here in the Land of the Midnight Sun;
Here in such beauty, hard not to have fun.

Only an hour away now, till landing I'm told;
Sit back and enjoy all, time today is like gold;
Goes by faster and faster, the older the chimes;
So enjoy it and use it, as by, passes the time.

As if God just reached down, parting clouds to allow;
A few peaks in the Brooks Range—we can recognize now;
The clouds have since risen, indeed higher today;
But the instrument approach will definitely clear the way.

My two friends in front, with maps 'cross their laps;
Loran, GPS[11], are to pilots: such excellent wraps;
For as blankets of wool, to the miners of old;
Approach plates and instruments, are to pilots as gold.

Up in Alaska, the North Pole 'tis near;
Up to Point Barrow, 'cause only it's there;
Up in the Land of the Midnight Sun;
Oh! To be here, and to have so much fun.

Life is so rich, but not of money I'm talking;
Just to be breathing, aware, and capable of walking;
Alive is as much, a function of the soul;
An attitude, not money, but better than gold.

Run down the descent check now, preparing for landing;
Cross check our instruments, so we end up there standing;
At the northernmost point of our United States;
'Tis a moment in time, my good fortune and fate.

Most landings are pleasant, and things of delight;
Best made when in daylight, and not in the night;
So today here at Barrow, of which we are near;
We'll fly 'neath the cloud deck, and land in the clear.

The Brooks Range is at six o'clock, that we've just passed;
The green trees of Alaska, for a time we've seen last;
To dip our toes into the Arctic so cold;
Unlike those before us, who were ever so bold.

---

[11]   Loran = *lo*ng *ran*ge navigation; GPS = *g*lobal *p*ositioning *s*ystem; both
means of air navigation

Land that is flat now, ahead and below;
'Tis hard to comprehend, Post and Rogers dying so;
Near where we are now, not up far ahead;
When their seaplane took off, and then came down like lead.

The story was told well, by a test pilot named Acord;
Whom we met in Fairbanks, when a museum we toured;
They were temporarily disoriented, as some pilots are;
But then sighted an Eskimo, standing on an ice bar.

They landed in the water, to get directions to Barrow;
In a lagoon out from town, about a dozen miles or so;
They then took off and crashed, their plane upside down;
Two legendary figures, lives over, and drowned.

Barrow

Barrow's a town, just a village remote;
Up hear on the edge of the wild North Slope;
Where Eskimo, Inupiat, have been here for centuries;
Today some Koreans, running restaurants, not many.

The Eskimos plied the Arctic, in small boats made of seal skin;
At their peril—to harpoon whales, in distant ocean they've been.
When visiting the shoreline, a few whale skulls you see;
Huge mandibles and maxilla bones—as long as some trees.

And, of course, you will find it, in far away places;
That wry sense of humor, that comes with small spaces:
For some time ago, there was a pole with fronds:
actually leaves of baleen;
So those who came to Barrow—could say, a "palm tree" they'd seen.

Polar bears occasionally, interrupt these nice folks;
Into the town, where they're considered no joke.
Other than that, the recreation seems fitting to be;
Confined mostly by teens, to riding their ATVs.[12]

In the summer o'er the horizon, the sun reigns for eighty-four days;
Makes for a life but unusual, in so many ways.
Don't think I'd get used to, either the summer or winter;
But enjoyed my visit, to the Inupiat Heritage Center.

---

[12]   ATV = all terrain vehicle

The memorial to Rogers and Post, is made of polished granite;
Presented by folks from Oklahoma—that state: another planet.
When looking at the names of people, who contributed
to this monument;
One of those noted, with one of our crew,
together to pilot training went.

So you see in the world of pilots, most are known to each other;
Perhaps not directly, but it's like a large group of fine brothers.
For quite a number in Alaska, have stopped to help us along;
Making certain that we take, no risks here that are wrong.

Greenies

I like greenies some, their balances and checks;
But not so much, as to have our economy wrecked.

Some are well intentioned, and do us all good;
Others have no life, and as protesters would;

Resort to tactics, that contribute little overall;
They march and travel so, responding to their call.

While journeying in Alaska, earlier this summer;
I went to the North Slope, and visited Point Barrow.

The greenies had been there, and will be back for sure;
I was told that and more, but the oil fields endure.

They apparently march, from one end of town to the other;
Creating a bit of publicity, and causing some bother.

But the question that most troubles me, one that I posed:
Just how do they get there? For all roads are quite closed.

In actuality, there are no through roads to Point Barrow;
So the greenies that go there, are not such straight arrows;

For they use planes and boats, just like you and me;
For them then I guess, that's the price of hypocrisy!

'Cause by walking or on sleighs, they most certainly don't go;
Yet they do their very best, to stop the Alaskan oil flow.

They march and they yell, as most protesters are wont;
Then again, just like you and me, they use the oil font.

They've perhaps done some good, of that I'm quite certain;
But I wish they'd slow down, or close their act's curtain;

For I've toured the huge oil fields at Prudhoe Bay;
An am pleased, indeed impressed, I must surely say.

The companies have been forced there, to clean up their act;
They are joined at the hip, with the state in their pact.

While like capitalists all, they're there for profits to make;
But the state government has made them take a high stake

In the preservation of tundra, and all the wildlife;
Seems now that the greenies could tune down their strife.

The people up in Alaska, as I now understand;
Want to run a gas pipeline, and with care surely can

Help those of us all, down in the Lower Forty-Eight;
Discontinue our reliance on Mideast oil, not having us wait:

To fill up our cars, heat our homes, watch prices rise high;
I'd rather see drilling on the North Slope—with wells not so dry.

So to tree huggers, tundra kissers, good and bad greenies all;
Let's use the North Slope of Alaska—please heed this call!

So we become less dependent on others who don't share:
The love of our country, those seeking not what is fair.

Some greenies would attempt to stop evolution in its tracks;
And for some, I think they only, want the dinosaurs back;

But when those greenies ride in boats, and arrive there by jets;
I somehow don't think that they understand hypocrisy yet.

Advertising Spin

For inevitably as the sun, arises on each morn;
Those coming to Alaska, would assuredly most scorn.
If the ad men had called Alaska—"land of the noon dark;"
Such words connote an image, has so little winning spark.

For all, 'tis so much better—known as Land of
the Midnight Sun;
Conjures up a portrait of people, having so much fun!
But the former term's like dirt, while the latter is but gold;
Therefore, far more tickets to come to Alaska, now are sold.

To Deadhorse And Prudhoe Bay

Now taking off from Barrow, it's wonderfully nice;
After trouble with a fuel pump, that Scott Moore fixed precise.
Heading east t'ward Deadhorse, we then steadily flew;
Whitewashed ice flows galore, sights abound that are new.

Just like in life, a problem here and there;
Fortunately for us three, we could get help where:
The land meets the Arctic, here bears they are white;
Ice and ocean to our left, tundra and lakes to our right.

That tundra looks foreboding, the ice looks far worse;
To go down there now, we'd definitely be cursed.
We're hugging the coast, in the whole day light;
'Neath the Midnight Sun, land knowing no night.

Up on the North Slope, we're having great fun;
Here in the Land of the Midnight Sun;
Wondrous sights all, to behold and see;
Those that God's made, for both you and me.

'Tis off to Deadhorse, we're flying today;
Just to see the oil fields, and Prudhoe Bay.
Passing Admiralty Bay, then Smith Bay next;
Flying IFR[13] now, as if by text.

---

[13]   IFR = *instrument* f*light* r*ules/* r*egulations*

The North Slope looks barren, devoid of all life;
Where water's near freezing; and ice flows are rife;
Unforgiving would be, for the unlucky soul;
Who showed no respect, and flew here like a fool.

'Tis great to have friends, up in front as today;
Two whom I respect, they are showing the way.
We're hugging the shoreline, wisps of clouds in the sky;
'Tis fantastic to be here, much better to fly.

Up on the North Slope, so beautiful here;
Traveling with good friends, so little to fear.
Up in the Land of the Midnight Sun;
Crossing land once again, but seeing nothing that runs.

The tundra looks fluid, so much like a swamp;
To land in the mush, I frankly don't want.
Cross Teshekpuk Lake now, so large with ice broken;
I feel small and alone—man is here, but a token.

But my friends are up front, two men I like most;
So we're sure not to end up, like Rogers and Post.
The granite in Barrow, today holds those names;
An unfortunate demise, an undesirable claim to fame.

At three thousand today, crossing terrain down below:
Cold water, ice and tundra—wanting not there to go;
It's grand to be flying, while not quite so high;
It's fine to be here, treasuring life's passing by.

Up near the North Pole, twelve hundred miles or so;
But en route to the Pole, doubt much different below;
Except the tundra no longer, reaches out to the Sea;
It's but ice and cold water, where polar bears be.

Up in the Land of the Midnight Sun;
Great to find towns, to have us some fun;
Grand to view sights—never seen such before;
Likely not to see them again, in this life, ever more.

But no doubt God's been here, and touched His hand
To this beautiful country, to this captivating land;
Up on the North Slope, where men drill for oil;
Up in the villages, where few Eskimos toil.

Here in the wilds of Alaska we fly;
For today there are few clouds, up in the sky;
A high layer above us, beginning to close;
But clear all around us, of most import off the nose.

A clear horizon encircling, from wing to wing;
The engine's running smoothly, as if it sings;
Beauty all 'round us, the lucky are we;
Here 'bove the tundra, and the Arctic Sea.

So much to see, at the Top of the World;
Behind us in Barrow, flags waved straight there, unfurled;
The wind blows crisply, a strong headwind today;
Holding us back some, hindering, our planned headway.

Just like in life, sometimes we're slowed down;
When it's certainly best then, to look all around.
Just like today—many options abound;
While it's flying we love, best to plan on the ground.

They say landings are good, those from which
you can walk away;
But landings are great, when the plane flies another day;
So many of life's lessons are learned in a plane;
But the foremost of all, pilots know that God reigns.

To be with us here, as we're up north to fly;
He's with us now, as patchy cloud puffs go by;
To be 'mongst us all, as we pass by each day;
God's with us past, present, and future—to stay.

Closing on Deadhorse, landing's at hand;
Up in Alaska, fantastic and grand.
Oil pumps are below us, currently sliding on by;
Runway's in sight now, as we plan leaving the sky.

While I think the greenies, most have it wrong;
I'm glad those who love nature, are somewhat strong.
What befuddles me most: is when protesters drive
Using oil that's drilled here, for their cars to imbibe.

Like many politicians, some greenies do go;
As hypocrites many, they sometimes do blow
Most surely to hear themselves, raise voices and speak.
I'm also quite glad, that most greenies are weak.

Up here in Alaska, most land undisturbed;
Up here in Alaska, where few are perturbed;
Up here in the Land of the Midnight Sun;
Deadhorse straight ahead, one night of more fun.

Leadership

To digress here is fine, for I need a short break;
The message below, for some they may take:

Just as in life, when following the leader;
The look stays the same, the views never change.
But leading the way, is most often easier;
Your decisions just yours, far and wide is the range.

So for pilots on whole, 'specially single seaters;
For those who've flown fighters, used FAC call signs too;
For those who've commanded aircraft, that signifies leaders;
For they, more than most, enjoy soaring the blue.

The moral of this story, is that of changing the view;
Not following the many, but joining the few
Who believe living life, is best controlled from in front;
Who'd rather pay that price, than just bearing the brunt

Of others' decisions, not generally to their liking;
Best to think for yourself—take the risk of being sent hiking;
What some have come to call, the issue of Indians and chiefs;
I'd rather lead than follow—that's my strong belief.

For those who go first, mostly have a clear view;
Not following as others, but leading as few.
Pilots have occasion, to lead more than most;
'Cause they seldom, if ever, have the freedom to coast.

Here today in Alaska, while flying on high;
Up here today, in the dazzling midnight sky;
The yellow today—not gold—is a sun that's so bright;
That turns night into day, 'tis shining and light.

Up in Alaska, in this beautiful sky;
Up on the North Slope, where it's so fun to fly;
Beware of weather, ice, and small passes, too;
But fly to Alaska, for the sights, fresh and new.

I'm glad I'm a pilot, for life's been much fun;
Flying's allowed me to soar, in the Land of the Midnight Sun.

Why "Deadhorse"?

When arriving in Deadhorse, you're struck by the name;
You wonder what the horse did—his acclaim to such fame.
Seems many who pass through here, ask the question of why;
As no horses have been here—to a latitude so high.

Then I came upon a news page, written by Deborah Bernard;
Of the *Prudhoe Bay Journal,* apparently researched quite hard.
She related that a miner, might have brought his horse here to stay;
But the mosquitoes drove it insane, as could occur even today.

Perhaps the "Crazyhorse Hotel," thus came by its name;
'Tis said then the horse, with a caribou, some blame;
Got together and joined, thus delighting the horse;
Could have happened, I guess—'cause up here, there's strange force.

Thus, the "Happy Horse Hotel," as a tribute to the pair;
But when winter hit, the horse died, though up here, 'tis quite rare.
But the story ends here, and is dispelled with some "facts;"
As Ms. Bernard's come forth, perhaps to better this act.

In days long ago, a very rich man, who in New York then lived;
For his son, set up a six million dollar trust fund—
to whom he wanted to give.
The crux of the issue, for the boy, while alive;
Could not get at the money, till he reached thirty-five.

So the young man, as others, ventured to the North Slope;
To spend a few years here, swapping time and energy for hope
That the money would start coming, to him while but playing;
Then he met some folks here, who owned gear for gravel hauling.

The boy talked his father, into co-signing a loan;
But shortly thereafter, the father but moaned;
'Cause the company then tanked, in danger of bankruptcy, you know;
So as "Deadhorse Haulers," he named it, for all of its woes.

And, of course, here again, the story departs;
As two tales but arise—so to give it more heart.
The first, most unlikely, has the company removing thence;
Dead horses from Fairbanks, called: "Deadhorse Haulers," since.

But the far more credible story, as currently, it's told;
From the father came forth, as the old tale unfolds;
"I hate to put money into feeding a dead horse," he said;
And, hence, the name stuck, as if it had lead.

So today, when visiting at Prudhoe Bay;
Most folks, like Ms. Bernard, prefer to say;
They like more that name, and not "Deadhorse," you see;
But it's better than Jackass Flats, Wyoming—as most would agree.

Prudhoe Bay

On the way from the plane, where on gravel we parked;
Picked up by a van from the hotel, we then embarked;
For the short trip to our digs, for the night we would stay;
As we rode, we listened to the driver, starting to say:

A grizzly was there, at the front door last night;
Left a huge paw print, right there in plain sight;
I thought I was being, reeled in, for certain;
'Cause I seriously doubted, these comments and version.

And when we arrived, we were shown the paw print;
Still doubted this tale, thought some veracity bent;
Checked in, got my key, and to my room I then went;
Only to shortly hear word, as through the hotel was sent.

A grizzly was just outside, much to my surprise;
Took my camera with others—all quite wide-eyed;
As he sauntered around, looking for grub;
Just a huge furry beast, fortunately then with no cub.

Next on our agenda was dinner, you see;
And with such a spread, we expressed our glee;
For up on the North Slope, the food, they don't spare;
Had all kinds of salads, entrees and more fare.

Then off for a short walk, over to the General Store;
Attacked by mosquitoes, don't think I've ever seen more;
They grow quite large here, and bashful they're not;
So I ran with some gusto, back to the room and my cot.

Pulled curtains down tight, to keep out the light,
As the Midnight Sun, this time of year, is so bright;
Got a good night's sleep, up early to eat;
Next to go on a tour, more wildlife to meet.

Return To Fairbanks

The weather's been spectacular, the temperatures mild;
Can't wait to get airborne now, just like a child!
Fifty degrees is unquestionably, a heat wave up here;
At Deadhorse and Prudhoe, where there's no alcohol or beer.

We're off just past noon, and we're climbing for air;
Might as well have been midnight, for all that we care.
Broken roughly with clouds o'er the range, they call Brooks;
Now forward t'ward another flight, can't wait to look!

Rolling down the asphalt, white stripes passing by;
My but it's fine, to be back in the sky!
A left turn to south, heading now for Fairbanks;
Showing care in the cockpit, there's no time for pranks.

Up in Alaska, where the flying's so pure;
Care shown to the checklist, for that's surely the cure;
For pilots demand of themselves, in order to be safe;
Good habit patterns, better, rather sooner than late.

Many hours of flying experience, 'tween the three of us, down below
In the Lower Forty-Eight, might as well, be just for show;
'Cause here in Alaska, as pilots, you need be alert;
For as aviators the world over, don't want to get hurt.

If you're coming up North, to travel by air;
You'll gain new experience, perhaps more than your share.
Use some caution, pay heed, to the locals up here;
And you'll most likely miss circumstances, that
you might otherwise fear.

Brooks Range at twelve o'clock, Deadhorse at six;
My but it's great to fly, not traveling with picks.
For today, we cover the ground, faster by far;
Not like the Eskimos, once traveling by stars.

We're entering some layers, of finely woven silk;
On instruments now, just as if in some milk;
Wisps of clouds all 'round us, cotton like balls;
Here up in the sky, we're now in God's halls.

Tundra below, small lakes all around;
Where caribou, arctic fox, and grizzlies abound.
The foothills are beginning, beneath us, to grow;
As we approach the Brooks Range, eleven thousand feet so.

We're leveling now, cumulus ahead, but thankfully no thunder;
In God's Holy Land, one can only just wonder:
How this grandest of wildness, came to be land;
Only choice that I know: by God's powerful hand.

Up in Alaska, freedom's the key;
It's great to be here, so nice to be me!
Up here in Alaska, where North Slope meets sea;
One can never forget, the creation by Thee.

If you have no religion, just come on up here;
See the wildlife, the Eskimos, vast dominion, so dear.
Here in the wonder, of this sacred land;
You'll see God's works, best of all, first hand.

Sun breaking through now, hard describing the bright;
Twenty-four by seven, holding back night;
Piercing through clouds, some blue sky so fine;
Appearing just now, o'er the horizon, on line.

Crossing the Brooks Range, jagged mountains below;
Good to be high now, no desire to be low;
For passes have crept up, and taken some souls
Of those who in weather, flew there, paid the toll.

Terrain below is unforgiving, like in Atigan Pass;
Such flights may be nice there, but might be your last:
The ground rising sharply, as it meets with the sky;
Some grasping for altitude, not sufficiently high.

As pilots from down, in the Lower Forty-Eight;
We fly up high, shun buzzing, not wanting to be bait
For those passes that have claimed now, more than a few;
Between us, thousands of flight hours, but here we are new.

Just like in life, show respect for new things;
And through such experiences, God surely brings
To pilots and others, alike, who explore;
Folks who, like us, will all always seek more.

Flying's like life, in so many ways;
I only hope that, I've got many more days
To see God's grandeur, so alive in the sky;
To pass through it all, as I fly on by.

Gold streaks of sunlight, appear as but strands;
If only in the sky, I could forever take my stand;
For I've loved to be here, a man long since once young;
Happiest to be where, in God's wonders—among.

For those hearty souls, who traveled to Alaska's coasts;
It's nice to be here now, to raise up a toast
To the miners, fishermen, whalers, Eskimos—all;
Who heard the Cry of the Wild, must have been such a call.

The Brooks' spires now reach up, from down just below;
For as we presently fly o'er them, ever so slow.
On to Fairbanks we wing now, a place for the night;
But in the Midnight Sun, we're always with light.

The fingers of ice, raise up ridges, so stark;
But few have climbed here, bet none on a lark;
Those bayonets of ice, cutting up steep slopes, so high;
Sheets and slivers of white, reaching aloft for the sky.

We're clearing the Range, to the south we now go;
Straight t'ward Fairbanks, from the backseat I know;
The two in the front seat, many hours with my friends;
Enjoying Alaska so fine, hope we'll pass through again.

Fairbanks in sight now, the runway's just off the nose;
Have traveled to Barrow, and Prudhoe, for repose;
Alaska has so many vast sights, to be seen;
I'm happy that God's let me, be here to glean.

A Father's Dream

One of my father's prime goals in this life;
Was to see Lake Louise, with his son and his wife;

He wasn't religious, as some seem to be;
But he made sure through God's wonders, I came to know Thee.

I hope my own children, through travel and verse;
Will come to realize, that life's but to rehearse;

For that life ever after, hope to find is divine;
Like gold in Alaska, life's lessons to mine.

MORE ON LIFE

There's a Pony in Here Somewhere

Dedicated to Robert M. "Bob" Glover whom I came to know when flying F-105's for seven years with the Virginia Air National Guard. Over the last 30 years I have watched in amazement as he has tackled virtually everything that life has thrown him with an excellent attitude that is without parallel. I have always admired the humorist Will Rogers. While I obviously did not have the pleasure of knowing the man, Bob Glover is most alike Will Rogers as any man I will ever know—quick witted and good humored.

When a friend of mine confronts troubles in life,
he often likes to say;
That a pony must be there with him, in the room
just eating hay.
'Cause it often feels when in the room, with manure
piling up so high;
And in many situations, he simply could not understand,
the why.

But my friend is an optimist—one of the greatest
with whom I've flown;
A fellow fighter pilot, one who's seen what few have known;
For he's cut a swath of southern pine, when tracking on a target;
And he's taken a large goose while low, passing through his cockpit.

So he's probably better than most, able with life's risks to assess;
That's why I listened carefully, when he told of the pony test.
When tasked with your life's problems, think as if you're in a room;
When it's coming past your eyeballs, way too late to use a broom

To sweep the troubles out the door, you should look fast for the pony;
'Cause when being kicked and in manure, 'tis not much ceremony.
So persevere and keep your head, just above the fertilizer;
For those who believe the pony's there, will be that much the wiser.

When you're being kicked in life, and your room is filling up;
Just smile and believe in the pony, using his thought as your backup!
When your problems all are gone, and you can hop
on that small horse;
It will take you to the next room, the ones waiting on life's course.

When the room then clears for all to see, and you get
upon that little beast;
The joy of it, the fun of it—your perspective in having put
such problems least.
So when you're being kicked in life, think you're down and out;
Try your best to find that pony, while looking all about.

And therein lies the moral—that a good attitude is always best;
When traveling through your life—it helps with all the tests.
So when that room begins to darken, with the stuff
that ponies bring forth;
If your problems are coming from the south,
do not just head but north;

Undertake them headfirst with a good outlook,
all that you can muster;
Tackling those difficulties, one at a time, not as if but in a cluster.
And if you do as my friend has done, most things in life will be bright;
He's one of the happiest folks I've known, keeping
all things quite light.

He's encountered more than a few of life's problems,
and overcome them all;
And when he's riding that pony, he's most certainly
having a ball!
'Cause if when problems are facing you down,
your attitude is great;
When there are no problems left, then
you've mostly controlled your fate.

Why the Sky is Blue

Dedicated to my good friend and room mate in Air Force pilot training in 1969-70, Bruce E. Happe. "Hap" is a captain with U.S. Airways and retired from service as a pilot in the U.S. Air Force and Air Force Reserves having flown C-130's and C-141's. He served in both Southeast Asia and Desert Storm. With two daughters he is not quite the chauvinist that the poem below would indicate as it relates to one of his many quips. And yes, for those who may wonder, I ran this attribution by him.

The sky above is most oft blue;

And on that subject, a friend offered a clue:

If God had wanted girls to fly;

He'd with His brush painted, pink through the sky.

On Becoming a Pilot

This story is told by many a pilot.

Way back, when I was but a little tike;
My parents wanted, for me many things.
And one of these, was to see planes in flight;
So I'd understand, the joy flying brings.

One day Dad took me, to an airport small;
To see all those slow planes, take off and land.
We had a grand time, such a wondrous ball
While watching them, and holding his strong hand.

I was so excited, while standing there;
I remember stating it, till this day;
That when I then grow up, no matter where;
I want to be a pilot, in some way.

Dad, a man of few words, as I recall;
Looked down, and smiled, but tightened his strong grip;
He said those goals were high and admirable;
And then he made a comment, not so flip:

He said a choice I'd have, could not do both;
If I wanted to become a flyer;
You cannot become an adult, he quoth;
If you want to pilot and soar higher!

My Donor Card

While passing through this life, I feel I've seen a bit;
And as I've gone along, I've tried to tackle most with wit.

And therefore as a result, should have been then no surprise;
When at the Division of Motor Vehicles, I eagerly cracked wise:

When the nice young lady asked me, while standing there in line;
If I would then consider, donating a valuable organ of mine;

I responded promptly—without the benefit of thinking very hard;
Asked if I could, in good conscience, list "scar tissue" on my donor card.

Dog Lovers' Delight

Dogs are indeed man's best friend. Since childhood I have had one almost continually by my side: "Koko" was a Boston bull dog who had to be put in another room before my dad could discipline me, and next was "Queenie," a Boxer whom we had for 15 years. Then there was service in Southeast Asia and "Lightning" was the mascot of the Night Rustics. Once married, we first got a beautiful Siberian Huskie, "Tasha," and had her for 13 years while our children grew up. She was followed by our most recent, a mutt rescued from the SPCA, whom we named "Chance"—as in No Chance, Second Chance, Fat Chance and Last Chance—a name that should see him through life.

I'm a lover of dogs, and most dignified to be such;
Likewise I don't like kittens and cats—all felines—very much.

It's best summed up in a saying, I might as well decree:
There are way too many cats, and not enough recipes.

Leonid's Shower

Thanks to a 3:45 AM wake up call one early morning by our good friends, Bob and Jan Glover, my wife and I, together with our daughter, Cheerie, joined the Glovers in their back yard to watch the splendid meteor shower that lasted for a few hours.

On the eighteenth of November, 'round four o'clock in the morn;
   Sparkles poured from the heavens, as if they had been torn;
Streaks of blaze in abundance, burning as they flew;
   Beginning as 'twas publicized—yes, just right on cue.

These intermittent strings of light, boring across the sky;
   A more brilliant display of beams, I don't want to see pass by.
This spectacle of brightness, soaring 'cross heaven's backdrop;
   Stardust appearing scattered around, as if swept by a celestial mop.

The luster and plenty, said to come, once in thirty-three years;
   Fortunate were we, such a cloudless morn, and ever then so clear.
The aura of the sky above, came forth with such an array;
   Appearing in every quadrant, 'fore God turned the night to day.

The glistening of the fireballs, the twinkle of their lights;
   Yet another example of God's power. Oh! Such luminous might!
What a stellar display of meteors, I've only before once seen;
   The night burst forth with glitter, a show by the stars convened.

When to Retire?

Determining when in life to retire;
Is a question for us all.
Wanting to do so before we expire;
To sit back and have a ball.

To do so before too soon—for sure;
Can create a money shortfall.
To retire when timely—for certain the cure;
Enough funds before the Call.

But retiring too late in life's quite sad;
Not sufficient time to play.
When such a decision proves then bad;
Little time left to while away.

So the trick's to manage both our time—
And our money along life's path.
To make resolutions both bold and sublime;
To avoid taking a financial bath.

Give then much thought as you work and plan;
Striving for much fun in life.
Both now so that in retirement you can;
Avoid life's pitfalls and strife.

Investment Decisions—
Easy versus Simple

When the market's going up and high;
    It's easy to get on the train.
        But when it's headed down—makes you cry;
           When's the time to get out of the rain?

When decisions and investments look easy;
    It's probably not the best time;
        To part with your money, when greedy;
           'Cause you'll lose more than a few dimes.

On the one hand, when it's simple;
    To grasp the concept or thought.
        Might be worth making a principle;
           Such an idea might be best bought.

So keep in mind the great difference;
    Between "simple" and "easy" as words.
        When choosing of those, "simple's" the preference;
           'Cause "easy" is for the birds.

God's Pulpit

As some need a Bible, others yearn for a group;
Most pilots I know, need only break through the soup;
To see land below, clouds all around;
Blue sky sometimes, we know He abounds.

Many pilots I know, to church they don't run;
Most pilots I know, have had all too much fun;
But when the last approach is coming into sight;
I know that most pilots will have understood His might.

For unlike most folks, who live life on the ground;
We've heard jet engines and props—do love those sounds;
And to most of us who've flown, with God all around;
For as pilots most have surely in God have found.

The sky's a religion, much like many to fuss;
But up here we fly, 'cause we know He's with us;
For such endless freedom, years ago I sought flight;
But today I'm content, just to see all His sights.

For to be up here now, in the wild blue yonder;
Is to but break the code on God's holy wonders;
To have come to grasp Him, as most pilots know;
Is for us so much better, than those far below.

I would trade not the sky, for a great congregation;
But would rather be up here, in His truest creation;
Unforgiving the sky is, much as it is in life;
But up here with my God, I've known so little strife.

Life's problems seem so trivial, indeed all quite so small;
When I'm up here in the sky, trying to take it in—yes, all;
Life's such a sweet and blissful trip, as it gradually unfolds;
A bold pilot once upon, now just gracefully growing old.

As I've grown older, hope wiser, I've come to know why;
God made the clouds, those forms in His azure sky;
The rain, wind and ice, that all, soon come to entice;
So that pilots like me and others, will love His works: so nice.

While most have had their feet
    —planted firmly on this earth;
The folks I've known who've flown the most
    —have had more than their share of mirth.

Not only pilots, but those who've fought, and others certainly so;
For those who've treated patients, yet others, as is truly though;
For firemen and police alike, paramedics, those who give their time;
For others whose only claim to fame, is layers of such grime;

But most of all the only mandate: is to firmly in Thee believe;
So to treasure life after death, when it comes time to take leave.

But it is fitting for those of us, who've lived mostly on the edge;
To have had much fun, enjoyed this life, and to in honesty allege;
As with those who've toiled along life's path, who solemnly have trod;
That we've all reached out and touched, the almighty face of God.

Luck

To those with luck who have it;
And to those without, who don't;
Comes oft to those when working hard
But to them that loaf, it won't.

Pay heed now, to these words
As they float across this page:
'Cause this plays for most who seek it;
While they glide across life's stage.

When you simply sit and watch for it;
Luck, most times, won't prevail;
Or show itself, for all its worth;
Life will appear for some, then stale.

But with those, who shoulder burdens
When working mightily, with life's loads;
Tis somehow fitting, when luck finds them
As they trod happily, along life's roads.

'Tis better to be a hunter then;
Than a trapper, who waits for luck.
'Tis better then, to move ahead;
While some others become, but stuck.

So give some thought to striking out;
At least, a few times, with life's toss;
As Babe Ruth then, once held that claim
To most at bats, with three good across.

The key to life, is that of getting up;
Each day, as the sun rises 'bove;
Suit up, and stand before life's plate;
Avoid hate, and seek those who love.

Be sure to take an occasional swing;
As life's balls fly across the plate.
At least you'll have moved much closer;
Then, to what many consider, but fate.

Go out, to find yourself, and thence
Of wisdom, you'll have your share.
Then put yourself to work, most hard;
Embracing life, with a hearty dare.

And then you'll come upon a pearl;
To share with those, who look for luck;
You generally find it, while striving;
Finds not those, who have no pluck.

So luck is what, you make of it;
As you open, life's great doors;
Go forth and savor, all you can;
Discover, what, life has in store.

And of all the words, of those once wise,
As you seek and toil for goals;
Remember more often, days than not;
You make your luck, as life unfolds.

Faith

For most men and women
In a religion they believe.

But what I cannot understand
Is that all too many take leave

Of their senses, and oaths
Their belief in love and peace

'Cause all too many seek to settle
Differences in wars that never cease.

The Irish Protestants fight the Catholics;
And the Arabs fight the Jews;

Some Islamics attack the Christians;
But those at peace, are all too few.

The Christians fought the Infidels;
Away back centuries past.

Now some followers of Mohammed
Are after Infidels to the last.

Makes little sense to me now
Who in God they profess to believe.

Have not most of those who choose to fight
Of their religion, simply taken leave?

Hope

Of all human faculties
We have with to cope;

The greatest in life
Is the feeling of Hope.

From birth to the grave;
Even with afterlife;

Hope springs eternal
To mitigate strife.

In young as with old;
Hope gives us our strength;

To help us rise up;
To take us the length.

Hope carries us forward
From lows to new highs;

Makes waking each morn
Fresh as life passes by.

Exciting becomes
The next breath that we take;

For Hope is our anchor;
As we strive for life's breaks.

Acknowledgments

I would like to especially thank my loving wife, Noreen, for reading all the poems, on occasion several times, while editing. That exercise began when I faxed my Eulogy to Don Hagle to her from Alaska. Her numerous thoughts on subject matter and rhythm have certainly contributed to and enhanced the end result. Our daughters, Noelle, Erin, and Cheerie, also assisted during a period of over six months in reviewing and typing many of the poems.

Lynette Hagle, the widow of my good friend Don, was very receptive to the Eulogy and Don's sister, Holly, read it at his funeral. Bob Harris, a fellow Rustic FAC, read a number of my initial poems and has lent support. My Class Agent from VMI, Walter Judd, has offered words of encouragement after having read several poems and posting one on the VMI web site. Also, Bill Harris, an F-105 pilot with whom I served in the Air National Guard and who flew over the North in the Thud, offered, as an author, suggestions as to publishing my poetry.

Through the use of word processing and email, drafts of poems were effortlessly sent back and forth between Alexandria and Virginia Beach during my traveling back and forth. The age that we live in is truly amazing.

Afterword

Writing poetry has given me a sense of inner peace and a newfound means of conveying a number of my feelings on a variety of subjects. It arises to, but will never reach, the joy of flying or watching my children grow and prosper.

One issue is most certainly projected though, my sense of humor—dry as it is. For that has gotten me through many of the difficulties that I have encountered in life. And for cat lovers, please take my "Dog Lovers' Delight" with the humor for which it was intended.

As I have grown older, I have enjoyed reflecting on many thoughts about life and I particularly treasured writing about Alaska. Everyone should travel there as it is one of the most vast and beautiful places on our earth.

Perhaps of far greater import, especially to me, is the work that I have begun on the subjects of Vietnam and Cambodia. I plan to continue in my efforts to depict the great variety of occurrences, many unique, and emotions experienced during that period in my life—some most serious and others quite lighthearted. After years of sidestepping many of the memories, I have decided to embrace them as they are, indeed, as much a part of me as anything.

That time, 1970-1971, was a period in our country's history, when, with many other young men and women, we shouldered the burdens of responsibilities unlike any others we would encounter in this life. It was, however, as a direct result of those obligations that, in all too many cases, our actions were weighed with heavy consequences.

To some degree the result of those who write it, much of history has not been kind to all who served our country in Southeast Asia or in the United States military during that period of time. Our troops back then did not enjoy the unfettered support that they thankfully do today.

Many volumes neglect or all but frown on the activities of many of us. The Rustic Forward Air Controllers (FACs)—the unit I served with—who guarded the skies over Cambodia and supported that country's troops during 1970-73 is but one example. That history has been virtually omitted from the written word until, within the last few years, the classified status was removed from most of our work there.

Other friends with whom I went to college or flew with in subsequent assignments have had their missions suffer a similar fate. Among these are the Covey FACs who supported Army and other insert/extract missions "out country" in Laos and Cambodia. A Brother Rat and friend, Paul Curs, for example, was awarded the Silver Star only within the last few years for a daring mission that saved American lives. Stories told by the Raven FACs in Laos also provide some hair raising tales.

There are many others who paid a price, whether physically or emotionally or both, for fighting to support our beliefs and our political dictates. To be sure there were many other FAC units, some in which friends of mine flew having call signs that included "Mike" (Jerry Coy), "Walt" (Roger Groff) and "Rash," those who supported the 1st Air Cav and lived next to us at Bien Hoa. These are to name but just a few FACs. And that does not begin to approach the over 3 million men and women who served there.

Flying is one of the greatest pleasures ever created. Orville and Wilbur most likely did not have the slightest clue as to the joy

that would be derived by millions of pilots—and some passengers—
in the future. We all owe them a vote of thanks, particularly given
the fact that we just celebrated the centennial of their first flight
on December 17, 1903. It is hard to believe that we are now
embarking on our second century of aviation.

There are simply no words or language to adequately describe
the delight and thrill of flying, especially when fast and low, or for
that matter, when low and slow and someone wants you in their
sights. You just have to experience it. Over the years I have strapped
on everything from a glider to a J-3 Cub to a supersonic T-38 to a
mach 2+ fighter, the F-105, and as added insurance, have made 8
parachute jumps, all of which were fortunately elective.

I have flown in some of the most serene of times and, for me,
in some of the most harrowing. Hopefully for those who now slip
the "surly bonds" of earth, they will enjoy more the former and
none of the latter. And perhaps in the coming years, I will be able
to provide further insight through my poetry and prose into the
wide range of experiences that flying affords.

Don Mercer
Virginia Beach